APPALACHIAN TRAIL GUIDE TO

Maryland and Northern Virginia
With Side Trails

1995
Fifteenth Edition

THE POTOMAC APPALACHIAN TRAIL CLUB
118 Park St., S.E.
Vienna, VA 22180

APPALACHIAN TRAIL GUIDE TO
MARYLAND AND NORTHERN VIRGINIA
Fifteenth Edition edited by
Jean C. Golightly

Printing History

The area covered in this *Guide* was originally part of a more comprehensive publication known as the *Guide to Paths in the Blue Ridge*. The first version was issued in 1931 and referred to Virginia only. In the second edition, in 1934, the area covered was extended to include Pennsylvania and Maryland; supplements were issued in 1935 and 1937. The third edition was published in 1941 and the fourth in 1950. In 1959, the comprehensive guidebook was divided into three sections, one of which covered the area represented by this *Guide*. The sixth through thirteenth editions appeared in 1966, 1970, 1972, 1974, 1984, 1986 and 1989 respectively. A second printing of the thirteenth edition, in 1991, adopted the present cover photo. A fourteenth edition was printed in 1993.

Library of Congress Catalog Number 86-62720
ISBN 0-915746-77-8

Copyright © by the Potomac Appalachian Trail Club
118 Park St., S.E.
Vienna, VA 22180

Cover: Black Rock Cliffs, Maryland
(photo by Michael T. Shoemaker)

ACKNOWLEDGMENTS

For the past ten years this guidebook has been faithfully and meticulously updated and revised by Michael T. Shoemaker. We thank him for his years of dedication.

The present book retains the same format and much of the same material as the previous edition. However, many Trail changes have occurred, especially in the Maryland section. Based on the most recent data, David Pierce has totally revised the Maryland portion of the book and updated segments of the northern Virginia section.

Jean Golightly
Editor

ABBREVIATIONS

AT or Trail	Appalachian Trail
ATC or Conference	Appalachian Trail Conference
mi	mile or miles
PATC	Potomac Appalachian Trail Club
USGS	U.S. Geological Survey
yd	yard or yards

A.T. *in Maryland*

CONTENTS

Raven Rock, Maryland

CHAPTER 1
USE OF THE GUIDE AND THE TRAIL

This *Guide* is one of a series of guidebooks that covers the entire Appalachian Trail (*AT*) from Maine to Georgia. It contains a general description and detailed data in both directions for 97.8 miles of the *AT*, from the Maryland-Pennsylvania border to Shenandoah National Park. A list of other guidebooks for the Trail appears on the back cover.

Disclaimer Notice to All
Trail Users and Landowners

Although the editor, the PATC, and ATC strive for accuracy and thoroughness in the materials published, it is impossible to ensure that all the information accurately describes the condition and location of the Trail. Consequently, the editor, the PATC and its agents, and the ATC expressly disclaim any liability for inaccuracies in this book.

The Trail crosses both private and public lands, the owners or administrators of which may alter Trail conditions and impose regulations on the use of the Trail. The editor, the PATC and its agents, and the Conference expressly disclaim any liability for the negligence, wrongful actions or omissions of any landowner with respect to the Trail, and of any Trail users with respect to private or public property.

This *Guide* and associated maps refer to springs as sources of water. The purity of water from any sources cannot be guaranteed, and the editor, the PATC and its agents, and the Conference expressly disclaim liability for any impurities in such water. Extreme care must be used in drinking such water. All water should be purified by boiling, or chemically treated before use, but even these measures will not guarantee the safe use of such water, particularly if the water is chemically polluted. Creeks, rivers, ponds, and lakes should never be used as a water source.

The editor, the PATC and its agents, and the Conference expressly disclaim any liability for the condition of the Trail and for all occurrences on the Trail.

Safety and Security

Although criminal acts are probably less common on the Appalachian Trail than in most other human environments, they do occur. Crimes of violence, up to and including murder and rape, have taken place over the years. It should be noted, however, that such serious crimes on the *AT* have a frequency rate on the order of perhaps one per year or less. Even if such events are less common on the Trail than elsewhere, they can be more difficult to deal with because of the remoteness of most of the Trail. When hiking, you must assume the need for at least the same level of prudence as you would exercise if walking the streets of a strange city or an unknown neighborhood.

A few elementary suggestions can be noted. Above all, it is best not to hike alone. Be cautious of strangers. Be sure that family and/or friends know your planned itinerary and timetable. If you customarily use a "Trail name," your home contacts should know what it is. Although telephones are rarely handy along the Trail, if you can reach one ask the operator to connect you to the State Police if you are the victim of, or a witness to, a crime.

The carrying of firearms is **not** recommended. The risks of accidental injury or death far outweigh any self-defense value that might result from arming oneself. In any case, guns are illegal on national parklands and in certain other jurisdictions as well.

In the meantime, be prudent and cautious, without allowing common sense to slip into paranoia.

Format of the Guidebook

The data in this *Guide* cover the Maryland Trail, Sections 1 through 7, beginning at Pen Mar in the north and extending to Harpers Ferry in the south. The data for the Northern Virginia Trail, Sections 1-6, begin at Harpers Ferry and end at the border of Shenandoah National Park in the south. The West Virginia Trail data has been combined with Virginia because that portion of the Trail weaves back and forth across their mutual border. One chapter has been devoted to general information about Harpers Ferry, West Virginia.

The data for each Trail section are divided into three parts. The first part includes general planning information. This material is arranged under individual headings in the following order, although not every section includes every heading:

Road Approaches and Parking
Points of Interest
Maps
Shelters/Camping/Campgrounds
Public Accommodations
Supplies
Brief Description
Side Trails
Detailed Trail Data

The "Detailed Trail Data", the guide to the actual footpath, is in two parts. Data are given first for walking north to south on the Trail, and then for walking south to north. A column of distances on the left gives the mileage from the start of the section to important points along the Trail. Each point is briefly described, followed by directions to the next point.

It should be remembered that descriptions can become obsolete very quickly as man or nature alters the landscape.

Trail Maps

Detailed maps of the *AT* are available for the entire area covered by this *Guide*. Their use is highly recommended.

The maps have been prepared by the Maps Committee of the PATC and are based on USGS maps. These 5-color, topographic maps indicate the route of the *AT* highlighted in contrasting color, side trails, shelters, cabins, highways, forest areas, and other major geographical features. Four PATC maps cover the *AT* in Maryland and northern Virginia. Maps 5 and 6 (both at 1:62,500 scale) are printed on the same sheet and are priced as one map. Map 7 is at 1:50,000 scale. Map 8 is at 1:62,500 scale. The area covered by each is as follows:

Map No.	State	Area
5	Maryland	Pen Mar to Turners Gap
6	Maryland	Turners Gap to Harpers Ferry
7	Va/W.Va	Harpers Ferry to Snickers Gap
8	Virginia	Snickers Gap to Chester Gap

The map panel in the "Meet the PATC" brochure provides a general overview of all PATC maps and is useful in determining highway approaches to the *AT*.

The relevant PATC map is indicated under "Maps" for each section of the *AT*. PATC maps are available, for a reasonable charge, from the PATC headquarters in Vienna,

Virginia, and various other distributors. These maps, like the *Guide*, are periodically revised. This edition of the *Guide* used the following map editions: PATC Map 5/6, Edition 14 (1995); PATC Map 7, Edition 11 (1994); and Map 8, Edition 11 (1993).

The relevant USGS 7.5 min. quadrangles (1:24,000 scale) are also indicated under "Maps" for each section of the *AT*. These may be purchased for $4.00 (1995 price) at the Maps Sales Office at USGS Headquarters in Reston, Virginia, or by mail from Map Distribution, US Geological Survey, Box 25286 Federal Center, Denver CO 80225. In most cases, the USGS maps do not depict the current *AT* or indicate side trails open to the public; therefore, these maps are not necessary for trail orientation. The USGS maps primarily are helpful to those wishing to study the detailed terrain and hydrological features of the area.

The Trail

Trail Markings

The *AT* is marked by white paint blazes and standardized plaques. In Harpers Ferry, however, the Park Service has banned markings along the town streets in the historic district.

The paint blazes (2" by 6") have been placed at frequent intervals along the Trail. A double blaze (two blazes, one above the other) is placed as a warning sign. It may indicate a turn or change in direction that might otherwise not be noticed.

Metal plaques with the *AT* insignia are placed at greater intervals. Maintained side trails are marked by blue blazes similar in size to the white blazes.

Important intersections are marked with wooden signs.

Trail Maintenance

The PATC is responsible for maintaining about 240 miles of *AT*, as well as blue-blazed side trails, from Pine Grove Furnace State Park in Pennsylvania through Shenandoah National Park. Within Maryland, PATC has assigned Sections 1 and 2 to the Mountain Club of Maryland (Baltimore), and Section 3 to Maryland Appalachian Trail Club of Hagerstown. In any case, all maintenance work is done by unpaid volunteers, usually with sub-sections assigned to individual overseers.

Trail Use

Although much of the Trail is on public property, some of it still crosses private land. Owners can, and sometimes do, order the *AT* off their property. Where this happens, the alternatives are often limited—sometimes only public highways. It is, therefore, *extremely important that private property rights be respected.*

Those using the *AT* or side trails should not damage natural or man-made property, litter, carry firearms, or use trail bikes. Particular care should be taken to avoid fires. Smoking is discouraged, and fires should be built only at designated campsites. Camping should be done only at such campsites. Horseback riding requires specific permission of property owners and is forbidden in many areas.

Trail Relocations

Always follow the marked Trail. If it differs from the guidebook's Trail description, it is because the Trail was recently relocated in the area, probably to avoid a hazard or undesirable feature or to remove it from private property. If you use the old Trail, you may be trespassing and generating ill will toward the Trail community.

Information on Trail relocations between guidebook revisions is reported in ATC's magazine, *Appalachian*

Trailway News, issued five times annually. Every effort has been made in this *Guide* to alert you to relocations that may occur. Do not follow new trails that are not blazed, because they may not yet be open to the public.

Bear Spring Cabin and Blackburn Trail Center

Bear Spring Cabin, in Maryland Section 5, is the only cabin open to the public within the area covered by this *Guide*. It is a one-room, log structure on 1½ acres of land donated to the PATC in 1939 by Harrison S. Krider. No more than six persons, including children, may use the cabin and surrounding area overnight. The cabin is provided with necessary equipment, including pans, dishes, cutlery, wood stove, blankets, mattresses, and bunks, but no lighting sources are available. All the user need bring is personal gear, additional bedding (usually a sleeping bag), lighting sources (flashlights or lanterns), and food. A *spring* and privy are nearby. For access, see Bear Spring Cabin Trail, under "Side Trails," Chapter 8.

The cabin is locked. Arrangements for use, for a small fee, may be made up to four weeks in advance by calling Cabin Reservations at PATC Headquarters (703-242-0315) between 7 p.m. and 9 p.m. Mon.-Thurs., or 12 to 2 p.m. Thurs. and Fri.

The Blackburn Trail Center (see Virginia Section 2) is available for use by PATC members, or groups, for a small fee. Reservations are required, and may be made up to one month in advance, but exclusive use of the Center is not guaranteed. Call Cabin Reservations (see previous paragraph) to make reservations and to obtain information about who will be using the Center on specific dates. The Center has a full-time caretaker from April through September, but is locked at other times. The neighboring Hodgson House has been converted into a primitive cabin that accommodates eight. It has beds and a wood stove, but no mattresses or other equipment. It is open all year and is free to *AT* thru-hikers.

Water

Carrying a canteen is necessary, and a one-quart canteen may not be enough, especially in dry seasons. The exertion of hiking, combined with water shortages, could lead to dehydration and increase fatigue, thus marring an otherwise enjoyable experience.

Although the *AT* may have sources of clean, potable water, any water source can become polluted. Most water sources along the Trail are unprotected and consequently very susceptible to contamination. All water should be purified by boiling, chemical treatment, or portable water filters before using. Take particular care to protect the purity of all water sources. Never wash dishes, clothes, or hands in the water source. Make sure food and human wastes are buried well away from any water source.

Weather

Heavy rainstorms are common in Maryland and northern Virginia. Tents should be thoroughly waterproof. A full-length poncho or rainsuit and pack cover are essential; a short rainjacket is insufficient.

In midsummer, avoid overexertion and protect your face, shoulders, and legs from sun.

Do not assume that winter weather in Maryland and northern Virginia will be mild. It can suddenly become extremely cold, with temperatures as low as zero degrees

Fahrenheit for extended periods, especially at higher elevations. Considerable snowfalls can occur. Although the Trail in Maryland and northern Virginia usually can be traversed throughout the year, winter weather (December through March) can make travel and camping particularly difficult.

Equipment

The basic equipment rule is, never carry more than you need. Some items should be with you on every hike: the guidebook and maps; canteen; flashlight, even on day trips; whistle; emergency food; tissues; matches and fire starter; multipurpose knife; compass; rain gear; proper shoes and socks; warm, dry, spare clothes; and a first-aid kit (see page 27).

Take the time to consult periodicals, books, employees of outfitter stores, and other hikers before choosing the equipment that is best for you.

Getting Lost

Stop, if you have walked more than a quarter-mile (1,320 feet or roughly five minutes of hiking) without noticing a blaze or other Trail indicator. If you find no indication of the Trail, retrace your course until one appears. The cardinal mistake behind unfortunate experiences is insisting on continuing when the route seems obscure or dubious. Haste, even in a desire to reach camp before dark, only complicates the difficulty. When in doubt, remain where you are to avoid straying farther from the route.

Hiking long distances alone should be avoided. If undertaken, it requires extra precautions. A lone hiker who suffers a serious accident or illness might be risking death if he has not planned for the remote chance of isolation. Your destinations and estimated times of arrival should be known to someone who will initiate inquiries or a search if you do not appear when expected. On long trips, reporting your plans and progress every few days is a wise precaution.

A lone hiker who loses his way and chooses to bushwhack toward town runs considerable risks if an accident occurs. If he falls helpless away from a used trail, he might not be discovered for days or even weeks. Lone hikers are advised to stay on the Trail (or at least on a trail), even if it means spending an unplanned night in the woods in sight of a distant electric light. Your pack should always contain enough food and water to sustain you until daylight, when a careful retracing of your steps might lead you back to a safe route.

Distress Signals

An emergency call for distress consists of three short calls, audible or visible, repeated at regular intervals. A whistle is particularly good for audible signals. Visible signals may include, in daytime, light flashed with a mirror or smoke puffs; at night, a flashlight or three small bright fires.

Anyone recognizing such a signal should acknowledge it with two calls—if possible, by the same method—then go to the distressed person and determine the nature of the emergency. Arrange for more aid, if necessary.

Most of the *AT* is used enough that, if you are injured, you can expect to be found. However, if an area is remote and the weather bad, fewer hikers will be on the Trail. In this case, it might be best to study the *Guide* for the nearest place people are likely to be and attempt to move in that direction. If it is necessary to leave a heavy pack behind, be sure to take essentials, in case rescue is delayed. In bad weather, a night in the open without proper covering could be dangerous.

Rabies

Though rarely encountered, some individual mammals in Maryland and northern Virginia harbor rabies and therefore pose a serious danger to hikers.

Although raccoons have been the primary carriers, foxes, dogs, bats, and other mammals are potential carriers. All wild mammals should be avoided. Animals may carry the disease even though they show no symptoms. Unusual behavior by mammals should be reported to the authorities.

Transmission of rabies can occur from virtually any contact, even indirectly, from an inanimate object. Therefore, a danger is posed by raccoons tampering with packs and equipment. The usual precautions for hanging all equipment, by a rope, from a tree, should be followed.

Medical help should be sought immediately by anyone who believes he, or she, has had contact, direct or indirect, with a rabid animal.

Pests

Rattlesnakes and copperheads are found in Maryland and northern Virginia. See page 25 for the recommended treatment of snakebites.

Ticks, chiggers, no-see-ums, mosquitos, and other insects could also be encountered. Carry repellent.

Poison ivy, stinging nettle, and briars grow along many sections of the Trail. Long pants are recommended. Trailside plants grow rapidly in spring and summer, and, although volunteers try to keep the Trail cleared, some places may be filled with dense growth by midsummer, especially where gypsy moths have destroyed the overstory vegetation.

Parking

Park in designated areas. If you leave your car parked overnight unattended, you may be risking theft or vandalism. Please do not ask Trail neighbors for permission to park your car near their homes.

Hunting

Hunting is prohibited in many state parks and on National Park Service lands—whether acquired specifically for protection of the Appalachian Trail or as part of another unit of the national park system. However, most of the boundary lines that identify these lands have yet to be surveyed. It may be very difficult for hunters to know whether they are on NPS Trail lands. Hunters who approach the *AT* from the side, and who do not know that they are on Trail lands, may also have no idea that the Trail is nearby. The Trail traverses several other types of landownership, including national forest lands and state gamelands, on which hunting is allowed as part of the multiple-use management plan (national forests) or specifically for game (state gamelands).

Some hunting areas are marked by permanent or temporary signs, but any sign is subject to vandalism and removal. The prudent hiker, especially in the fall, makes himself aware of local hunting seasons and wears blaze orange during that time.

Trail Ethics

Improper use can endanger the continuity of the Trail. Please follow a few basic guidelines:

Do not cut, deface, or destroy trees, flowers, or any other natural or constructed feature.

Do not damage fences or leave gates open.

Do not litter. Carry out all trash. Do not bury it for animals or others to uncover.

Do not carry firearms.

Be careful with fire. Extinguish all burning material; a forest fire can start more easily than many realize.

In short: Take nothing but pictures, leave nothing but footprints, kill nothing but time.

Dogs are often a nuisance to other hikers. The territorial instincts of dogs often result in fights with other dogs. Dogs also frighten some hikers and chase wildlife. If a pet cannot be controlled, it should be left at home; otherwise, it will generate ill-will toward the Appalachian Trail and its users. Also, many at-home pets' muscles, foot pads, and sleeping habits are not adaptable to the rigors of *AT* hiking.

Keep to the defined Trail. Cutting across switchbacks, particularly on graded trails, disfigures the Trail, complicates route-finding, and causes erosion. The savings in time or distance are minimal; the damage is great. In areas where log walkways, steps, or rock treadway indicate special trail construction, take pains to use them. These have been installed to reduce trail-widening and erosion.

Group Hikes and Special Events

Special events, group hikes, or other group activities that could degrade the Appalachian Trail's natural or cultural resources or social values should be avoided. Examples of such activities include publicized spectator events, commercial or competitive activities, or programs involving large groups.

The policy of the Appalachian Trail Conference is that groups planning to spend one or more nights on the Trail should not exceed 10 people, and day-use groups should not exceed 25 people, unless the local maintaining organization has made special arrangements to both accommodate the group and protect Trail values.

C&O Canal Towpath

CHAPTER 2
FIRST AID ALONG THE TRAIL

by Robert Ohler, M.D., and the
Appalachian Trail Conference

Hikers encounter a wide variety of terrain and climatic conditions along the Appalachian Trail. Prepare for the possibility of injuries. Some of the more common Trail-related medical problems are briefly discussed below.

Preparation is key to a safe trip. If possible, every hiker should take the free courses in advanced first aid and cardiopulmonary-resuscitation (CPR) techniques offered in most communities by the American Red Cross.

Even without this training, you can be prepared for accidents. Emergency situations can develop. Analyses of serious accidents have shown that a substantial number originate at home, in the planning stage of the trip.

Think about communications. Have you informed your relatives and friends about your expedition: locations, schedule, and time of return? Has all of your equipment been carefully checked? Considering the season and altitude, have you provided for water, food, and shelter?

While hiking, set your own comfortable pace. If you are injured or lost or a storm strikes, stop. Remember, your brain is your most important survival tool. Inattention can start a chain of events leading to disaster.

If an accident occurs, treat the injury first. If outside help is needed, at least one person should stay with the injured hiker. Two people should go for help and carry with them notes on the exact location of the accident, what has been done to aid the injured, and what help is needed.

The injured will need encouragement, assurances of help, and confidence in your competence. Treat him gently. Keep him supine, warm, and quiet. Protect him from the weather with insulation below and above him. Examine him carefully, noting all possible injuries.

General Emergencies

Back or neck injuries: Immobilize the victim's entire body, where he lies. Protect head and neck from movement if the neck is injured, and treat as a fracture. Transportation must be on a rigid frame, such as a litter or a door. The spinal cord could be severed by inexpert handling. This type of injury must be handled by a large group of experienced personnel. Obtain outside help.

Bleeding: Stop the flow of blood by using a method appropriate to the amount and type of bleeding. Exerting pressure over the wound with the fingers, with or without a dressing, may be sufficient. Minor arterial bleeding can be controlled with local pressure and bandaging. Major arterial bleeding might require compressing an artery against a bone to stop the flow of blood. Elevate the arm or legs above the heart. To stop bleeding from an artery in the leg, place a hand in the groin and press toward the inside of the leg. Stop arterial bleeding from an arm by placing a hand between the armpit and elbow and pressing toward the inside of the arm.

Apply a tourniquet only if you are unable to control severe bleeding by pressure and elevation. Warning: This method should be used only when the limb will be lost anyway. Once applied, a tourniquet should only be removed by medical personnel equipped to stop the bleeding by other means and to restore lost blood. The tourniquet should be located between the wound and the heart. If there is a traumatic amputation (loss of hand, leg, or foot), place the tourniquet two inches above the amputation.

Blisters: Good boot fit, without points of irritation or pressure, should be proven before a hike. Always keep feet dry while hiking. Prevent blisters by responding early to any discomfort. Place adhesive tape or moleskin over areas of developing redness or soreness. If irritation can be relieved, allow blister fluid to be reabsorbed. If a blister forms and continued irritation makes draining it necessary, wash the area with soap and water and prick the edge of the blister with a needle that has been sterilized by the flame of a match. Bandage with a sterile gauze pad and moleskin.

Dislocation of a leg or arm joint is extremely painful. Do not try to put it back in place. Immobilize the entire limb with splints in the position it is found.

Exhaustion is caused by inadequate food consumption, dehydration and salt deficiency, overexertion, or all three. The victim may lose motivation, slow down, gasp for air, complain of weakness, dizziness, nausea, or headache. Treat by feeding, especially carbohydrates. Slowly replace lost water (normal fluid intake should be two to four quarts per day). Give salt dissolved in water (one teaspoon per cup). In the case of overexertion, rest is essential.

Fractures of legs, ankles, or arms must be splinted before moving the victim. After treating wounds, use any available material that will offer firm support, such as tree branches or boards. Pad each side of the arm or leg with soft material, supporting and immobilizing the joints above and below the injury. Bind the splints together with strips of cloth. Transport the victim to a medical facility for treatment.

Shock should be expected after all injuries. It is a potentially fatal depression of bodily functions that is made more critical with improper handling, cold, fatigue, and anxiety. Relieve the pain as quickly as possible. Do not administer aspirin if severe bleeding is present; Tylenol or other non-aspirin pain relievers are safe to give.

Look for nausea, paleness, trembling, sweating, or thirst. Lay the hiker flat on his back, and raise his feet slightly, or position him, if he can be safely moved, so his head is down the slope. Protect him from the wind, and keep him as warm as possible. A campfire will help.

Sprains: Look or feel for soreness or swelling. Bandage and treat as a fracture. Cool and raise joint.

Wounds (except eye wounds) should be cleaned with soap and water. If possible, apply a clean dressing to protect the wound from further contamination.

Chilling and Freezing Emergencies

Every hiker should be familiar with the symptoms, treatment, and methods of preventing the common and sometimes fatal condition of *hypothermia*. Wind chill and/or body wetness, particularly aggravated by fatigue and hunger, can rapidly drain body heat to dangerously low levels. This often occurs at temperatures well above freezing. Shivering, lethargy, mental slowing, and confusion are early symptoms of hypothermia, which can begin without the victim realizing it and, if untreated, can lead to death.

Always keep dry, spare clothing and a water-repellent windbreaker in your pack, and wear a hat in chilling weather. Wet clothing loses much of its insulating value, although wet wool is warmer than other wet fabrics. Always, when in chilling conditions, suspect the onset of hypothermia.

To treat this potentially fatal condition, immediately seek shelter and warm the entire body, preferably by placing it in a sleeping bag and administering warm liquids. The addition of another person's body heat may aid in warming.

A sign of *frostbite* is grayish or waxy, yellow-white spots on the skin. The frozen area will be numb. To thaw, warm the frozen part by direct contact with bare flesh. When first frozen, a cheek, nose, or chin can often be thawed by covering with a hand taken from a warm glove. Superficially frostbitten hands sometimes can be thawed by placing them under armpits, on the stomach, or between the thighs. With a partner, feet can be treated similarly. Do not rub frozen flesh.

Frozen layers of deeper tissue beneath the skin are characterized by a solid, "woody" feeling and an inability to move the flesh over bony prominences. Tissue loss is minimized by rapid rewarming of the area in water slightly below 105 degrees Fahrenheit (measure accurately with a thermometer).

Thawing of a frozen foot should not be attempted until the patient has been evacuated to a place where rapid, controlled thawing can take place. Walking on a frozen foot is entirely possible and does not cause increased damage. Walking after thawing is impossible.

Never rewarm over a stove or fire. This "cooks" flesh and results in extensive loss of tissue.

Treatment of a deep freezing injury after rewarming must be done in a hospital.

Heat Emergencies

Exposure to extremely high temperatures, high humidity, and direct sunlight can cause health problems.

Heat cramps are usually caused by strenuous activity in high heat and humidity, when sweating depletes salt levels in blood and tissues. Symptoms are intermittent cramps in legs and abdominal wall and painful spasms of muscles. Pupils of eyes may dilate with each spasm. The skin becomes cold and clammy. Treat with rest and salt dissolved in water (one teaspoon of salt per glass).

Heat exhaustion, caused by physical exercise during prolonged exposure to heat, is a breakdown of the body's heat-regulating system. The circulatory system is disrupted, reducing the supply of blood to vital organs such as the brain, heart, and lungs. The victim can have heat cramps and sweat heavily. Skin is moist and cold with face flushed, then pale. Pulse can be unsteady and blood pressure low. He may vomit and be delirious. Place the victim in shade, flat on his back, with feet 8-12 inches higher than head. Give him sips of salt water—half a glass every 15 minutes—for about an hour. Loosen his clothes. Apply cold cloths.

Heat stroke and *sun stroke* are caused by the failure of the heat-regulating system to cool the body by sweating. They are emergency, life-threatening conditions. Body temperature can rise to 106 degrees or higher. Symptoms include weakness, nausea, headache, heat cramps, exhaustion, body temperature rising rapidly, pounding pulse, and high blood pressure. The victim may be delirious or comatose. Sweating will stop before heat stroke becomes apparent. Armpits may be dry and skin flushed and pink, then turning ashen or purple in later stages. Move victim to cool place immediately. Cool the body in any way possible (*e.g.*, sponging). Body temperature must be regulated artificially from outside of the body until the heat-regulating system can be rebalanced. Be careful not to overchill once temperature goes below 102 degrees.

Heat weakness: Symptoms are fatigue, headache, mental and physical inefficiency, heavy sweating, high pulse rate, and general weakness. Drink plenty of water, find as cool a spot as possible, keep quiet, and replenish salt loss.

Sunburn causes redness of the skin, discoloration, swelling, and pain. It occurs rapidly and can be severe at higher elevations. It can be prevented by applying a commercial sun screen; zinc oxide is the most effective. Treat by protecting from further exposure and covering the area with ointment and a dressing. Give the victim large amounts of fluids.

Artificial Respiration

Artificial respiration might be required when an obstruction constricts the air passages or after respiratory failure caused by air being depleted of oxygen, such as after electrocution, by drowning, or because of toxic gases in the air. Quick action is necessary if the victim's lips, fingernail beds, or tongue have become blue; if he is unconscious; or if the pupils of his eyes become enlarged.

If food or a foreign body is lodged in the air passage and coughing is ineffective, try to remove it with the fingers. If the foreign body is inaccessible, grasp the victim from behind, and with one hand hold the opposite wrist just below the breastbone. Squeeze rapidly and firmly, expelling air forcibly from the lungs to expel the foreign body. Repeat this maneuver two to three times, if necessary.

If breathing stops, administer artificial respiration, as air can be forced around the obstruction into the lungs. The mouth-to-mouth, or mouth-to-nose, method of forcing air into the victim's lungs should be used. The preferred method is:

1. Clear the victim's mouth of any obstructions.
2. Place one hand under the victim's neck and lift.
3. Place heel of other hand on the forehead, and tilt head backwards. (Maintain this position during procedure.) Use thumb and index finger to pinch nostrils.
4. Open your mouth, and make a seal with it over victim's mouth. If the victim is a small child, cover both the nose and the mouth.
5. Breathe deeply, and blow out about every five seconds, or 12 breaths a minute.
6. Watch victim's chest for expansion.
7. Listen for exhalation.

Lyme Disease

Lyme disease is carried by *Borrelia burgdorferi,* a spirochete form or bacteria, and is transmitted by the bite of a deer tick, an insect the size of this period. These ticks feed during one stage of their life cycle on deer, but they can also be found on birds, field mice, and other rodents.

Hikers should be aware of the symptoms and monitor themselves and their partners for signs of the disease. Inspect for tick bites at the end of each day, wear light-colored clothing so you can spot and brush off ticks; if you are bitten by a tick, remove the tick immediately by grasping it as close to the skin as possible with tweezers and tugging gently. If the tick's head has attached under the skin, douse insect with rubbing alcohol or touch with a hot match. When treated early, Lyme disease usually can be cured with antibiotics.

The early signs of Lyme disease are a rash at the site of the tick bite with a red circle and a clear center, flu-like symptoms, such as sore throat, severe fatigue, chills, headaches, fever, muscle aches, stiff neck, appetite loss, nausea, vomiting, diarrhea, and abdominal cramps. However, one-quarter of all people with an infected tick bite show none of the early symptoms.

If the disease is not treated in its early stage, serious complications involving the heart, joints and nervous system, may appear months or years later. These symptoms may be arthritic complications such as hot, swollen and painful joints, muscles, tendons and shooting pains in the arms and legs. Heart complications such as irregular heartbeat, chest pain, fainting, dizziness, and shortness of breath, also become evident. Neurological complications may arise, such as facial paralysis, abnormal skin sensations and sensitivities, insomnia, and hearing loss. The psychological complications, including mood changes, memory and concentration problems, depression and dementia, are often mistaken for mental

illness. Lyme disease can also be misdiagnosed as rheuma-
toid arthritis, meningitis, or multiple sclerosis. The disease
is rarely fatal, but heart complications may cause life-
threatening arrhythmias, and infection during pregnancy may
cause miscarriage.

It may be necessary to contact a university medical
center or other research center if you suspect you have been
bitten by an infected tick. It is not believed people can build
a lasting immunity to Lyme disease, although vaccines are
being tested. A hiker who has contracted and been treated for
the disease should still take precautions.

Lightning Strikes

Although the odds of being struck by lightning are low,
200 to 400 people a year are killed by lightning in the United
States. Respect the force of lightning, and seek shelter during
a storm.

Do not start a hike if thunderstorms are likely. If caught
in a storm, immediately find shelter. Hard-roofed automobiles or large buildings are best; tents and convertible
automobiles offer no protection. When indoors, stay away
from windows, open doors, fireplaces, and large metal
objects. Do not hold a potential lightning rod, such as a
fishing pole. Avoid tall structures, such as ski lifts, flag-
poles, powerline towers, and the tallest trees or hilltops. If
you cannot enter a building or car, take shelter in a stand of
smaller trees. Avoid clearings. If caught in the open, crouch
down, or roll into a ball. If you are in water, get out. Spread
out groups, so that everyone is not struck by a single bolt.

If a person is struck by lightning or splashed by a charge
hitting a nearby object, the victim will probably be thrown,
perhaps a great distance. Clothes can be burned or torn.
Metal objects (such as belt buckles) may become hot, and
shoes can be blown off. The victim often has severe muscle

contractions (which can cause breathing difficulties), confusion, and temporary blindness or deafness. In more severe cases, the victim may have feathered or sunburst patterns of burns over the skin or ruptured eardrums. He may lose consciousness or breath irregularly. Occasionally, victims stop breathing and suffer cardiac arrest.

If someone is struck by lightning, perform artificial respiration and CPR until emergency technicians arrive or you can transport the injured to a hospital. Lightning victims may be unable to breathe independently for 15 to 30 minutes but can recover quickly once they can breathe on their own. Do not give up early; a seemingly lifeless individual can be saved if you breathe for him promptly after the strike.

Assume that the victim was thrown a great distance; protect the spine, treat other injuries, then transport him to the hospital.

Hantavirus

The trail community learned in the fall of 1994 that—18 months earlier—an A.T. thru-hiker had contracted a form of the deadly hantavirus about the same time (June 1993) the infection was in the news because of outbreaks in the Four Corners area of the Southwest. After a month-long hospitalization, he recovered fully and came back to the A.T. in 1994 to finish his hike.

Federal and state health authorities tested various sites in Virginia that fall—looking for infected deer mice, the principal carriers in the East—but found no mice infected with the virus, which apparently is most often picked up when it is airborne. (The virus travels from an infected rodent through its evaporating urine, droppings and saliva into the air.)

Predictably enough, that was just the sort of thing to hit the newspapers and trigger anxieties among some hikers. However, the health authorities said they themselves would worry more about rabies—never a report of that on the Trail. Hantavirus is extremely rare and difficult to "catch." Prevention measures for thru-hikers are relatively simple: Air out a closed, mice-infested structure for an hour before occupying it; don't sleep on mouse droppings (use a mat or tent); don't handle mice; treat your water; wash off your hands if you think you have handled droppings.

If you are truly concerned about hantavirus, call ATC for a fact sheet.

Snakebites

Hikers on the Appalachian Trail may encounter copperheads or timber rattlesnakes on their journey. These are pit vipers, characterized by triangular heads, vertical elliptical pupils, two or less hinged fangs on the front part of the jaw (fangs are replaced every six to ten weeks), heat-sensory facial pits on the sides of the head, and a single row of scales on the underbelly by the tail.

The best way to avoid being bitten by poisonous snakes is to avoid their known habitats and reaching into dark areas (use a walking stick to move suspicious objects). Wear protective clothing, especially on feet and lower legs. Do not hike alone or at night in snake territory; always have a flashlight and walking stick. Do not handle snakes. A dead snake can bite and envenomate you with a reflex action for 20 to 60 minutes.

Not all snakebites result in envenomation, even if the snake is poisonous. The signs of envenomation are one or more fang marks in addition to rows of teeth marks, burning pain, and swelling at the bite (swelling usually begins within five to ten minutes of envenomation and can become very severe). Lips, face, and scalp may tingle and become numb 30 to 60 minutes after the bite. (If these symptoms are immediate and the victim is frightened and excited, then they are most likely due to hyperventilation). Thirty to 90 minutes after the bite, the victim's eyes and mouth may twitch, and he may have a rubbery or metallic taste in his mouth. He may sweat, experience weakness, nausea and vomiting, or faint one to two hours after the bite. Bruising at the bite usually begins within two to three hours, and large blood blisters may develop within six to ten hours. The victim may have difficulty breathing, have bloody urine, vomit blood, and may collapse six to 12 hours after the bite.

If someone you are with has been bitten by a snake, act quickly. *The definitive treatment for snake-venom poisoning is the proper administration of antivenom. Get the victim to a hospital immediately.*

Keep the victim calm. Increased activity can spread the venom and the illness. Retreat out of snake's striking range, but try to identify it so the authorities can estimate the amount of antivenom necessary.

Immediately transport the victim to the nearest hospital. If possible, splint the body part that was bitten, to avoid unnecessary motion. If a limb was bitten, keep it at a level below the heart. ***Do not apply ice directly to the wound.*** If it will take longer than two hours to reach medical help, and the bite is on an arm or leg, place a 2"x 2", 1/4"- thick cloth pad over the bite and firmly wrap the limb (ideally with an elastic wrap) directly over the bite and six inches on either side, taking care to check for adequate circulation to the fingers and toes. This wrap may slow the spread of venom.

First-Aid Kit

The following kit is suggested for those who have had no first-aid or other medical training. It costs about $15, weighs about a pound, and occupies about a 3" x 6" x 9" space.

Eight 4" x 4" gauze pads   Five 2" bandages
Four 3" x 4" gauze pads   Ten 1" bandages
Six alcohol prep pads   One tweezers
Ten large butterfly closures   One 3" x 4" moleskin
One triangular bandage (40")   One small scissors
Two 3" rolls of gauze
Twenty tablets of aspirin-free pain killer
One 15' roll of 2" adhesive tape
One 3" Ace bandage
Twenty salt tablets
Three safety pins
Personal medications as necessary

References

Red Cross first-aid manuals.

Mountaineering First Aid: A Guide to Accident Response and First Aid (Seattle: The Mountaineers, 1985).

Emergency Survival Handbook, by the American Safety League (1985). A pocket-sized book and survival kit with easy instructions.

Medicine For the Outdoors: A Guide to Emergency Medical Procedures and First Aid, by Paul S. Auerbach, M.D. (Boston: Little Brown, 1986.)

Backpackers on A.T.

CHAPTER 3
THE APPALACHIAN TRAIL

The Appalachian Trail (*AT*) is a continuous, marked footpath extending 2,157 miles along the crest of the Appalachian mountain range from Katahdin, a granite monolith in the central Maine wilderness, south to Springer Mountain in Georgia .

The Trail traverses mostly public land in 14 states. Virginia has the longest section, with 536 miles, while West Virginia has the shortest, less than 20 miles along the Virginia-West Virginia boundary and a short swing into Harpers Ferry at the Maryland border. The highest elevation along the Trail is 6,643 feet at Clingmans Dome in the Great Smoky Mountains. The Trail is only slightly above sea level near its crossing of the Hudson River in New York.

Credit for establishing the Trail belongs to three leaders and countless volunteers. The first proposal for the Trail to appear in print was an article by regional planner Benton MacKaye of Shirley, Massachusetts, entitled, "An Appalachian Trail, a Project in Regional Planning," in the October 1921 issue of the *Journal of the American Institute of Architects*. He envisioned a footpath along the Appalachian ridge line where urban people could retreat to nature.

MacKaye's challenge kindled considerable interest, but at the time most of the outdoor organizations that could participate in constructing such a trail were east of the Hudson River. Four existing trail systems could be incorporated into an *AT*. The Appalachian Mountain Club (AMC) maintained an excellent series of trails in New England, but most ran north-south; the Trail could not cross New Hampshire until the chain of huts built and operated by the AMC permitted an east-west alignment. In Vermont, the southern 100 miles of the Long Trail, then being developed in the Green Mountains, were connected to the White Mountains by the trails of the Dartmouth Outing Club.

In 1923, a number of area hiking clubs that had formed the New York-New Jersey Trail Conference opened the first new section of the *AT*, in the Harriman-Bear Mountain section of Palisades Interstate Park.

The Appalachian Trail Conference (ATC) was formed in 1925 to stimulate greater interest in MacKaye's idea and to coordinate the clubs' work in choosing and building the route. The Conference remains a nonprofit educational organization of individuals and clubs of volunteers dedicated to maintaining, managing, and protecting the Appalachian Trail.

Although interest in the Trail spread to Pennsylvania and New England, little further work was done until 1926, when retired Judge Arthur Perkins of Hartford, Connecticut, began persuading groups to locate and cut the footpath through the wilderness. His enthusiasm provided the momentum that carried the Trail idea forward.

The southern states had had few trails and even fewer clubs. The "skyline" route followed by the *AT* in the South was developed largely within the new national forests. A number of clubs were formed in various parts of the southern Appalachians to take responsibility for the Trail there.

Perkins interested Myron H. Avery in the Trail. Avery, who served as chairman of the Conference from 1931 to 1952, enlisted the aid and coordinated the work of hundreds of volunteers who completed the Trail by August 14, 1937, when a Civilian Conservation Corps crew opened the last section (on the ridge between Spaulding and Sugarloaf mountains in Maine).

At the eighth meeting of the ATC, in June 1937, Conference member Edward B. Ballard successfully proposed a plan for an "Appalachian Trailway" that would set apart an area on each side of the Trail, dedicated to the interests of those who travel on foot.

Steps taken to effect this long-range protection program resulted first in an October 15, 1938, agreement between the National Park Service and the U.S. Forest Service for the promotion of an Appalachian Trailway, through the relevant national parks and forests, extending one mile on each side of the Trail. Within this zone, no new parallel roads would be built or any other incompatible development allowed. Timber cutting would not be permitted within 200 feet of the Trail. Similar agreements, creating a zone one-quarter mile in width, were signed with most states through which the Trail passes.

After World War II, the encroachments of highways, housing developments, and summer resorts caused many relocations, and the problem of maintaining the Trail's wilderness character became more severe.

In 1968, Congress established a national system of trails and designated the Appalachian Trail and the Pacific Crest Trail as the initial components. The National Trails System Act directs the secretary of the interior, in consultation with the secretary of agriculture, to administer the Appalachian Trail primarily as a footpath and protect the Trail against incompatible activities and the use of motorized vehicles. Provision was also made for acquiring rights-of-way for the Trail, both inside and outside the boundaries of federally administered areas.

In 1970, supplemental agreements under the act—among the National Park Service, the U.S. Forest Service, and the Appalachian Trail Conference—established the specific responsibilities of these organizations for initial mapping, selection of rights-of-way, relocations, maintenance, development, acquisition of land, and protection of a permanent Trail. Agreements also were signed between the park service and the various states, encouraging them to acquire and protect a right-of-way for the Trail outside federal land.

Slow progress of federal efforts and lack of initiative by some states led Congress to strengthen the National Trails System Act. President Jimmy Carter signed the amendment, known as The Appalachian Trail Bill, on March 21, 1978.

The new legislation emphasized the need to protect the Trail, including acquiring a corridor, and authorized $90 million for that purpose. With less than 150 miles unprotected by 1988, this project is expected to be completed soon.

In 1984, the Interior Department formally delegated the responsibility for managing the *AT* corridor lands outside established parks and forests to the Appalachian Trail Conference. The Conference and its clubs retain primary responsibility for maintaining the footpath, too.

The Conference publishes information on constructing and maintaining hiking trails, official *AT* guides, and general information on hiking and trail use.

The Conference membership consists of organizations that maintain the Trail or contribute to the Trail project and individuals. ATC membership provides a subscription to *Appalachian Trailway News*, published five times a year, and 15-percent discounts on publications. The Conference also issues two newsletters, *The Register*, for Trail maintainers, and *Trail Lands*, for contributors to its land-trust program, the Trust for Appalachian Trail Lands. Annual membership dues range from $18 to $30, with life memberships available for $500 (individual) or $750 (couple).

Membership forms and a complete list of publications are available from the Appalachian Trail Conference, P.O. Box 807, Harpers Ferry, W. Va. 25425, (304) 535-6331. The office is open nine a.m. to five p.m. (Eastern Time), Monday through Friday, and nine to four on weekends from mid-May through October.

CHAPTER 4
GEOLOGY ALONG THE TRAIL
by Collins Chew

The Appalachian Mountains have a long and fascinating history. Much that is known about geology and mountains was discovered through the study of the long, often straight, ridges in this area. If the Appalachian Mountains are thought of as a book, several interesting chapters may be read by observant people hiking along the Appalachian Trail in Maryland and northern Virginia.

Another mountain range stood "here" before the Appalachians. "Here" meaning that the rocks of those ancient mountains now lie under much of Eastern North America. The continent then, 1.1 billion years ago, was south of the equator. (The surface of the earth is made up of a number of thin, relatively rigid "plates," which move about the earth's surface at the speed our fingernails grow, an inch or two each year.) At that time, the North American Plate collided with (probably) the western side of the South American Plate, and the mountains formed as the two plates slowly crushed into each other. Those old rocks have been heated and changed several times; they are coarsely crystalline (crystals visible to the naked eye) with white minerals (mostly quartz and feldspar) and dark minerals (often mica and hornblende). Often the minerals are found in light and dark bands that show how a hot, somewhat softened, rock flowed slowly like putty at great depth and under intense pressure. Great movements since that time have left large, generally narrow slivers of that rock in place within the Appalachian Mountains. It so happens that one short section of the Appalachian Trail crosses a narrow band of this 1.1 billion-year-old rock around Sandy Hook Bridge, between Weverton Cliffs and Maryland Heights. The Trail here follows the towpath of the old Chesapeake & Ohio Canal, and little if any of the old rock can be seen, but the adjacent Pleasant Valley lies on these rocks that once lay under ancient mountains.

No records were left here for several hundred million years as those mountains eroded away. About 800 million years ago, the great land mass began to pull apart into separate continents again. During the next 200 million years, faults broke up the land, and mountain-size areas tilted, sank, or rose. Great outpourings of dark, very fluid, basalt lava formed extensive sheets of black rock. A few explosive volcanoes erupted lighter lava and ash. Records of this time, centered about 700 million years ago, are found in those old lava flows, although chemical changes have altered the black basalt to greenstone, a dark gray-green rock. In many places, this dark rock breaks along straight lines at sharp angles, which gives the rock a very craggy appearance. The rock weathers to clayey soil containing rock chips. These old lava flows are found from the northern edge of Tennessee to Pennsylvania. They lie under the Appalachian Trail of Maryland and northern Virginia in short sections at the trail to Buzzard Knob, at Foxville Road, from Washington Monument State Park to Turners Gap, and in spots between Wilson Gap and Ashby Gap. The southern 23 miles of this section, from Ashby Gap to Shenandoah National Park, is on this dark rock. Darker spots and holes in the rock show where minerals filled former gas bubbles in the molten rock. White quartz and light green epidote are found in the spots and in veins that make striking lines in the dark rock. Between Wolfsville Road and Raven Rock Road is a short section underlain by red volcanic rock typical of the explosive volcanoes.

An ocean somewhat like the Atlantic Ocean formed to what is now the east. It is called the Iapetus Ocean. Erosion wore away the mountains of North America, and the rocks cooled, became denser, and sank lower in the crust. The shallow sea at the edge of the ocean gradually covered the continent, and a sand beach formed along the shore. Eventually additional deposits covered the sand and turned it into hard quartzite, which still shows the sand grains and pebbles from which it formed. In many places, lines in the rock show where little sand bars grew. Each tide or rain washed a little more sand over the edge to make a new layer. These beds, which lie at an angle to the general bedding plane of the rock, are called crossbeds. The quartzite is extremely hard and resistant to erosion. White quartz veins create striking elongated patterns in the quartzite. These veins formed as deposits from solutions that flowed through cracks after the main body or rock had been laid down.

Generally found under ridges, the quartzite underlies all of the Appalachian Trail in this area except at the locations mentioned above and in Harpers Ferry, West Virginia. Many cliffs are composed of this quartzite, which appears more blocky than the greenstone. It weathers to sand. In places the ridge is flat, and it is puzzling why it is not farmland. The answer lies in the relatively sterile sand, which holds few nutrients and little water. In some locations, streaks of sand alternate with black humus. The sand and humus do not seem to mix well. Even in the absence of surface rock, the change of bedrock from quartzite to greenstone can be noticed where the surface sand gives way to dirt and clay containing rock chips. Some small beds of shale (formed from hardened mud) do lie within the quartzite, but they are infrequently obvious along the *AT*. These rocks formed about 550 million years ago.

As the sea grew deeper, clear water covered the sand, and limestone formed over it. Occasionally mud washed in from the center of the continent. Although limestone and mud covered large areas of the Eastern United States, it is evident in only one place in our section of the *AT*. Beds laid down as mud were changed to slate, which shows in Harpers Ferry and as ledges in the rivers there. Earth movements imparted a wavy pattern to some of the slate near the town. This is the youngest rock under the *AT* in this area and is over 500 million years old.

The Iapetus Ocean narrowed as part of the crust sank at an angle under other crust, and islands were brought against North America. These islands of a land called Avalon became much of the Piedmont Plateau to the east of the *AT*. Erosion of these new eastern lands covered our area with deep layers of sand and mud. Later, perhaps 250 million years ago, North Africa slowly collided with North America, crushing a large area of these sediments, causing once flat beds to become rippled in huge folds and sliding some areas over others as great faults broke the rock. To the south, tens of miles of rock layers slid over others in a manner likened to roof shingles being pushed over one another. The beds of rocks under the Appalachian Trail here were turned to steep angles or were even overturned. Relative to each other, the rocks have had little movement since that time. The beds now tend to line up nearly in a north-northeast to south-southwest direction.

Since then, erosion averaging perhaps an inch per thousand years has removed thousands of feet of rock to expose the surface we see today. The more resistant beds (most frequently quartzite) erode at slower rates and are left as ridges, whereas the limestones and shales erode to the valleys that parallel the *AT*. Greenstone varies somewhat from place to place and can be fairly resistant. It forms some of the mountains. The long ridges generally trace the upturned edges of quartzite. One side of the ridge may parallel the upper surface of the quartzite and have at the top a cliff that faces the other side of the mountain. The hardest quartzite is relatively thin, and softer rock underlies it. When this softer rock erodes from under the quartzite, the top edge breaks off and rolls down the mountain, leaving the cliff. In places in Maryland, the *AT* follows the level surface of a shelf beside the cliff. This is an unusual feature, common only in Maryland and nearby Pennsylvania. The relatively even tops of the ridges were once thought to be the remains of a level plain, called a peneplain, but it is now thought that the quartzite erodes too fast to be the remnant of a plain that existed millions of years ago. Nevertheless, gradual uplift has sustained the mountains' elevation, although periods of slower uplift may have let erosion predominate and allowed the mountains to be nearly eroded away for a time. These periods of unchecked erosion may have contributed to the comparatively even ridgetops; however, the changing rates of uplift and erosion are not very well understood. It is thought that uplift and erosion are nearly balanced now, so that the mountains maintain a nearly constant elevation.

Almost 200 million years ago, Africa (and, to the north, Europe) began to pull away from North America. By 160 million years ago, a narrow Atlantic Ocean had appeared. (It continues to grow wider as measured by satellites.) New ocean floor formed as black basalt lava oozed out of cracks along the Mid-Atlantic Ridge. The nearby ocean became the low point and provided short steep paths along which new rivers washed away sediment from the mountains. The Potomac River drained a particularly large area, and its power allowed it to cut the deep canyon we see at Harpers Ferry. The Shenandoah River was originally a small tributary of the Potomac. In flowing into the deep gorge of the Potomac, however, the Shenandoah cut down swiftly and enlarged its valley until it captured the headwaters of many other smaller streams that once crossed the Blue Ridge and flowed directly into the Atlantic Ocean. The low points of the ridge—such as Keys Gap, Ashby Gap, and Chester Gap—once held streams that flowed across the Blue Ridge. After the Shenandoah River captured their headwaters, the slow uplift overcame erosion and lifted the gaps above the surrounding valleys.

In the last few million years, great ice sheets have occasionally advanced from the north, but they never quite reached our area. (They did reach central Pennsylvania.) The freezing times helped break up the rocks and, in a few places, the frost heave action caused rocks to separate by size. This led to the formation of boulder fields such as the Devils Racecourses, which resemble, and are called, "rock rivers." These boulder fields once moved slowly and may yet be moved a bit by ice that forms under them. Lichens, and later trees, grow on these rocks as the movement stops.

The topography we see today resulted from a long period of erosion working on the very slowly rising land, a process that accentuated the differences in rocks with differing resistance. This process continues today.

CHAPTER 5
MARYLAND

GENERAL INFORMATION
Distance: 39.8 Miles

The *AT* follows the crest of South Mountain, a name
applied to a succession of narrow ridges, from the Pennsylvania line to the Potomac River. Along the river, the Trail is
located on the old Chesapeake & Ohio Canal towpath, now
part of the Chesapeake & Ohio Canal National Historical
Park. From the towpath, the Trail crosses the Potomac on
the Goodloe Byron Memorial Footbridge. The continuation
of South Mountain across the river, known as Short Hill
Mountain, dwindles and becomes indistinguishable among
the low foothills of northern Virginia. The Trail is therefore
located on a parallel ridge to the west, Blue Ridge Mountain,
which forms the boundary between Virginia and West
Virginia. Similarly, the extension of Blue Ridge Mountain
into Maryland is known as Elk Ridge, which continues north
as far as Crampton Gap. Both Elk Ridge and South Mountain
are part of the Blue Ridge Mountains of Maryland.

South Mountain is mostly covered with hardwoods, and
the slopes drain into the tributaries of the Potomac. The
numerous viewpoints along the Trail include Pen Mar, High
Rock, Black Rock Cliffs, Annapolis Rocks, Monument
Knob, White Rocks, Crampton Gap, and Weverton Cliffs.
South of Monument Knob, the Trail is rich in Civil War
history.

In Maryland, the elevation of South Mountain varies from
930 feet at Crampton Gap, to about 1,880 feet on the
southwest slope of Quirauk Mountain. Lambs Knoll, 1,772
feet, dominates the southern part of the ridge.

The Maryland portion of the Trail has been divided into the following sections:

1. Pen Mar to Raven Rock Hollow .... 5.8 mi
2. Raven Rock Hollow to Wolfsville Road .... 3.5 mi
3. Wolfsville Road to Interstate 70 .... 8.3 mi
4. Interstate 70 to Turners Gap .... 5.0 mi
5. Turners Gap to Crampton Gap .... 7.2 mi
6. Crampton Gap to Weverton .... 6.7 mi
7. Weverton to Harpers Ferry .... 3.3 mi

Since South Mountain is now a state park along its entire length in Maryland, camping is permitted *only* in designated areas and open fires *only* in fireplaces provided. See the following list:

0.2/39.6	Pen Mar Park (See Shelter/Camping, Section 1, Maryland, for exact location.)
4.9/34.9	Devils Racecourse Shelter
9.4/30.4	Hemlock Hill Shelter
13.7/26.1	Pogo Memorial Primitive Campsite
17.1/22.7	Pine Knob Shelter
22.8/17.0	Dahlgren Back Pack Campground
24.5/15.3	Rocky Run Shelter (seasonal spring)
29.4/10.4	Crampton Gap Shelter
37.3 /2.5	Weverton Primitive Camp (no water)

GROUP CAMPING: Any group of more than ten persons planning to camp in South Mountain State Park should call or write in advance to: Supt. of South Mountain State Park, 900 Arnoldtown Road, Jefferson, MD 21755. Phone: 301-293-2420.

HISTORY ALONG THE TRAIL

The rich history and colorful folklore of the Trail in Maryland compensate for its lack of spectacular scenic grandeur.

Early History

South Mountain served as a barrier that contributed to a pattern of north and south migration by the aborigines. Unlike the open country of the western plains and eastern ridges of the Rocky Mountains, where the edges of open ridges provided the safest travel for the Indians, the crest of South Mountain was not used by the Indians according to tradition. The Indians followed the Monocacy Trail from Pennsylvania, crossing the Potomac at Noland's Ferry. The Monocacy Trail is sometimes called the Warriors Path. On the west side of South Mountain, the Delaware Indians in the north and the Catawbas from the south followed the Antietam and Conococheague Creek valleys, crossing the Potomac at their deltas. Here their battles continued after the arrival of the first white men. In the 1730s and 1740s, these valleys became the corridors for German immigrants arriving in the port of Philadelphia bound for the Shenandoah Valley and other parts of Virginia where Lord Fairfax offered inducements for settlement.

A few trappers and settlers crossed South Mountain in the 1720s and 1730s. Israel Friend was mining ore on both sides of the Potomac near the mouth of Antietam Creek in the late 1720s, and a few settlers were farming along Antietam Creek in the 1730s. By 1732, the Lord Proprietor (Lord Baltimore) caused surveys to be made and began to grant lands on the west side of South Mountain. Comparative safety from the Indians awaited the Treaty of Lancaster in 1744, followed by the purchase of land from the Indians by the colony of Maryland. The Treaty of Lancaster with the Six Nations permitted the Indians to travel through Maryland from Pennsylvania to the Carolinas and established a temporary boundary between Maryland and Pennsylvania as far west as two miles above the source of the Potomac. For three hundred pounds sterling, the Indians provided a quit claim to lands east of this location.

Locations of Early Crossings of South Mountain

The earliest traverse of the South Mountain barrier in Maryland seems to have been along the Potomac, where neutral territory was maintained by the Indian tribes during the spring run of the yellow suckers. This gap through the Blue Ridge became the earliest thoroughfare of explorers and trappers. Louis Michelle and an exploring party from Annapolis crossed here in 1707. By 1733 Peter Stephens was operating ferries across both the Potomac and Shenandoah rivers at this gap in the Blue Ridge, and Peter Hoffman, a peddler from Baltimore, was making stops at the Stephens trading post on his route between Frederick and the German settlements in the upper Shenandoah Valley. A foldboat for use on western rivers was produced in the government shops at Harpers Ferry and collected by the Lewis and Clark Expedition (1804-1806) at the beginning of their trip. Later the canal and railroad followed the wagon road when the settlers pushed westward toward the Ohio. Both were in operation in this section by the end of 1834.

The first road to cross the ridge to reach the frontier was Israel Friend's Mill Road through Crampton Gap. The crossing through Turners Gap was a foot and horse path until General Braddock's army built a road in 1755 for his wagon train and personal carriage. Passenger stagecoach service across the gap was inaugurated on August 1, 1797. Several sessions of the Maryland legislature provided funds for the improvement of the road; in 1806 Turners Gap was designated the route of the National Road, and Federal improvements followed. By the 1850s, traffic on the National Road had declined, with the railroads and canal absorbing the freight and passenger traffic.

Old South Mountain Inn at Turners Gap, which still operates as a tavern (meals and drinks), is one of the oldest public houses along the *AT*. The date of the first tavern in Turners Gap cannot be determined, but the construction of the present building has been estimated as early as 1732 and as late as 1780. It had 22 rooms to rent, and at the height of the traffic on the National Road it employed blacksmiths to repair wagons and shoe horses around the clock and kept relay horses in the stables to relieve those exhausted from the steep grade. Abraham Lincoln spent a night at the tavern while on his way to take his seat in Congress, and it was reportedly a favorite hangout of Daniel Webster and Henry Clay. Presidents Jackson, William Henry Harrison, Polk, Taylor, and Van Buren passed through Turners Gap when traveling the National Road, and some of them may have stayed overnight in the tavern.

Mrs. Dahlgren, widow of Admiral John A. Dahlgren, commandant of the Washington Navy Yard during the Civil War and credited with perfecting the rifled cannon, bought the tavern in 1876 for a summer home, retaining the name, South Mountain House. She was shocked by the "corruption" of Christian doctrine among the people of South Mountain. She exposed their corrupted beliefs and described their poverty-stricken lives in a book published in 1882. For her missionary work among them, she built the Gothic stone chapel that overlooks the Trail. Restored by Mr. Griffin, 1963-5, the chapel is open on Saturdays, Sundays, and holidays from 1 to 5 p.m.

The Sisters of St. Mary's of Notre Dame used the South Mountain House for a summer retreat from 1922 until 1925, when the property was again sold for commercial purposes. A dancing pavilion was added where the veranda is now located, and at one time "the tavern served as a full-blown brothel." Mitchell H. Dodson purchased the property in 1957. The stucco was removed from the stone facings, and the original fireplaces were uncovered.

Mason and Dixon Line

The Mason and Dixon Line, the boundary between Maryland and Pennsylvania, should not be overlooked. During the summer of 1765, Charles Mason and Jeremiah Dixon, British astronomers and surveyors, crossed with a small army of chainbearers, local surveyors, axmen, rodmen, cooks, and other laborers. A supporting road westward was constructed to transport supplies and equipment.

The boundary had been in dispute since the grant was made to William Penn in 1681. Lord Baltimore's colonists called the Pennsylvanians "Quaking Cowards," and the latter referred to the Catholics of Maryland as the "Hominy Gentry." The descendants of William Penn and George Calvert, the first Lord Baltimore, agreed to abide by a line that would be surveyed by the two reputable scientists, Mason and Dixon, who were then observing the transit of the planet Venus from a position in Africa. At the time of the survey, a line separating slave-holding colonies from the north was not contemplated, although it came to pass that Dixie, or Dixieland, became the name for the area south of the Mason and Dixon Line.

To mark the boundary line between the two colonies, milestones and, at five-mile intervals, crownstones were placed. Milestone No. 91 is the closest to the Appalachian Trail, but it is inaccesibly located on private land in Pen

Mar. A nearby crownstone is No. 90, one mile east (as the crow flies), in the village of Highfield. These stones are made of limestone and were transported from England to the land underlain with limestone.

Industry

Whiskey making was perhaps the first industry along the Trail in Maryland. With the many sources of spring water on the slopes of South Mountain, corn, rye, and wheat grown in the valleys were made into whiskey, which was cheaper to ship to market then the bulkier grain. When a Federal tax was placed on whiskey in 1794, the distillers of South Mountain joined their compatriots in western Pennsylvania in the Whiskey Rebellion. A march on Frederick disbanded when the rebels learned that 500 Federal troops were waiting for them there.

Whiskey distilling continued into the late 1800s at Smithsburg on the northwest slope of South Mountain and at Burkittsville on the east slope of Crampton Gap. At Burkittsville in the 1880s, the Needwood Distillery (Golden Gate Whiskey) and Ahalt's Distillery were competitors. Both advertised using spring water from South Mountain. For aging and a better flavor, J. D. Ahalt shipped his whiskey to Rio de Janiero and back. Outerbridge Horsey made a better arrangement. After aging in his 3,000-barrel brick warehouse, his Golden Gate whiskey was shipped around the Horn to San Francisco for storage for a year before it was returned to Burkittsville, where it was again aged before sale.

Moonshining along the lower end of South Mountain and adjacent ridges of the Blue Ridge reached an advanced stage during Prohibition, when Spencer Weaver organized the moonshiners into a syndicate for production and marketing.

Inducements for moonshiners to join his syndicate included a steady income and "cradle to the grave" fringe benefits.

Moonshiners were paid a monthly salary plus a production incentive based upon a unit price for whiskey delivered. If the occupational hazard of a raid resulted in a jail term for the moonshiner, the salary continued, and loans for capital equipment, repayable from later production proceeds, were made available for the re-establishment of the moonshiner in business.

Weaver provided a widow's pension in the event of an accidental death of the moonshiner, and he also had a standing arrangement with a funeral home in Harpers Ferry to cover burial costs. Spencer Weaver used the former Salty Dog Saloon across the Potomac from Harpers Ferry for the base of his operations. But prosperity may have ruined Weaver; he started drinking his own product, and mild heart attacks followed. One night he backed his auto into the C&O Canal and was found dead.

Iron-making became an important industry near South Mountain, where there were trees to burn for charcoal. The Frederick Forge of the 1750s became the Antietam Ironworks after Washington County was formed from Frederick in 1776. Catoctin Furnace was located to the northeast, Mount Aetna to the northwest, Keep Tryst near Harpers Ferry, and the Blue Ridge Ironworks at Knoxville. The installations at Harpers Ferry were heavy consumers of charcoal.

The effect of the iron furnaces on South Mountain were twofold. First, they provided employment for charcoal burners on South Mountain, and second, the denuding of the slopes by burning the hardwoods for charcoal caused erosion and contributed to the floods of the Potomac in the 19th century. A tannery, which operated for approximately 100 years at Burkittsville, also contributed to the erosion by buying tanbark stripped from chestnut and oak trees. Some of the charcoal burners remained behind on the mountain, eking out a meager existence into the 20th century.

Weverton was an unsuccessful industrial town despite its natural advantages. Casper W. Wever, after a successful career as a highway and railroad construction engineer, used his savings to purchase land and water rights and construct industrial buildings to found the town of Weverton. Wever favored the railroad over the canal and opposed a right-of-way through his property for the canal company. (When most of his buildings lay idle, he refused to lease space for a temporary hospital for canal workers who had contracted Asiatic cholera in the epidemic of 1833.) Wever believed that the drop of 15 feet in the Potomac above Weverton was sufficient to provide water power to turn 300,000 textile spindles (one source estimated 600,000). In 1834 he started construction on industrial buildings for leasing and on a diagonal dam across the Potomac for diverting water into his millrace to provide power for the buildings.

It was reported that Wever's lease charges were too high and the buildings were not constructed to meet the specifications of small factories. Only two buildings were leased, one for marble cutting and the other by a company that made files for the national armory in Harpers Ferry. The Weverton enterprise failed before the Civil War.

The springs at Weverton have always been important to the community. Scharf refers to a hotel at Weverton built in 1796, which burned before 1880, and which was one of the first hotels in the country to offer rooms with running water for ladies and gentlemen. The replacement hotel built in 1880 also had running water. The sons of the last owner, Harry G. Traver, remember that the water was piped from the spring down the hill to the hotel, and that the water was used to cool beer and watermelon in the hotel, which then catered to railroad workers. The hotel site was where Md 67 connected with US 340 before the 1964-65 relocation. The hotel was razed for the road construction in 1916.

Weverton has been without industry since the Trail was built, and even the railroad station, where steam locomotives puffed on the siding while taking on water, was dismantled during World War II.

The Chesapeake and Ohio Canal is now a historical park administered by the National Park Service. Intersecting the Appalachian Trail, it provides a comparatively level path along the Potomac for 184.5 miles from Washington to Cumberland. Operation came to an end in 1924 when a flood damaged its structures. It had operated at a loss for many years, and the low traffic did not warrant sizable new capital expenditures for repairs and improvements.

Civil War and Memorial Arch to War Correspondents

More words have been devoted to South Mountain in the Civil War than to any other subject along the *AT* in Maryland. In addition, metal tablets in Turners and Crampton gaps provide details on troop movements during the Battle of South Mountain. Briefly, the Battle of South Mountain, September 14, 1862, was the curtain raiser for the Battle of Antietam or Sharpsburg. Finding lost Orders No. 191 revealed to the Union Command General Lee's orders to split his army into four segments and the routes for the three task forces detailed to capture Harpers Ferry, by-passed by the Confederates in the northern invasion. Union forces, superior in number and equipment, moved slowly and met strong resistance from small Confederate holding forces entrenched where the *AT* crosses Turners, Fox, Crampton and Brownsville gaps.

The Confederate command post was in the South Mountain Inn at Turners Gap. The delay permitted the three task forces under Stonewall Jackson to capture Harpers Ferry and allowed the Confederates to regroup on the west side of

Antietam Creek, where the two armies fought each other to a standstill. Three days of fighting, beginning on South Mountain, resulted in the highest casualty rate of the war.

A Civil War correspondent, George Alfred Townsend, returned to South Mountain after the war, and in 1884, flush with the proceeds from his books of fiction and syndicated newspaper articles on the Washington scene (he was the Drew Pearson of the post-Civil War period), he bought Crampton Gap and constructed a home, a house for his wife, a hall, a library, a lodge, a guest house, servants' houses, stables and a tomb for himself, where he was not buried. He called his estate "Gathland," "Gath" being his nom de plume. The buildings, mostly constructed of stone, were vandalized and only a wing of Gath Hall has been restored. The arch, dedicated in 1896 as a memorial to Civil War correspondents and artists, survives intact.

The 50-foot high memorial dominates Crampton Gap and frames the Catoctin Valley. It faces toward two other battlefields, Gettysburg and Winchester. The arch contains many inscriptions, and mythological figures are recessed in the stonework.

The off-balance arch has been described as an architectural cross between a Moorish arch and the tower on an old Frederick fire company station. The Hagerstown version is that Townsend adapted his architecture from the front of the Antietam Fire Co. building across from the B&O Railroad Station (now demolished for a parking lot) in Hagerstown, where Townsend observed the off-balance arch while awaiting transportation to his estate.

The arch is under the administration of the National Park Service, while the surrounding 135-acre park, Gathland State Park, is administered by the Maryland Department of Natural Resources.

Monument to George Washington

Monument to George Washington

The first monument to George Washington to be completed is on Monument Knob north of Turners Gap. The observatory, 30 feet high and constructed of native stone, is shaped like an old-fashioned cream bottle. Here gathered citizens from Boonsboro on July 4, 1827, "to spend the day at hard labor. An aged survivor of the Revolution delivered an address and at its conclusion a cold collation was spread," according to an early reporter. The people of the South Mountain area like ceremonies, and this monument and the one in Crampton Gap have been rededicated several times. Restored by the CCC in 1934-35, the monument is the focus of Washington Monument State Park, which has picnicking facilities.

Resorts

A few resorts flourished along the Appalachian Trail in Maryland. The first Black Rock Hotel, believed to have been built shortly after the Civil War, burned in 1880. After being rebuilt in 1907, the occupancy period was short. South Mountain Inn in Turners Gap advertised itself as a summer resort from 1852 to 1859 after the drop in traffic on the National Road.

The popularity of Pen Mar near the Pennsylvania line more than compensated for the lackluster of other resorts. At the turn of the century, the area supported seven hotels and about 100 boarding houses. A Lutheran picnic drew 15,000 to Pen Mar Park, and 5,000 was not uncommon on a summer day, when it was known as the Coney Island of the Blue Ridge. Special trains with several sections were scheduled by the Western Maryland Railroad from both east and west. Families were encouraged to spend the summer at

Pen Mar while the breadwinners commuted to Baltimore, Hagerstown, and Waynesboro, which was connected with Pen Mar by trolley. The Blue Mountain House, a rambling three-story frame structure, accommodating 400 overnight guests, featured 50-cent Sunday dinners. It was built in 1883 and burned in 1913.

The Western Maryland Railroad opened Pen Mar Park in 1878 to promote passenger traffic and supplement railway income. Promotional publicity for the park claimed the observatory on High Rock could hold 500 people on its three tiers. The amusement park was leased to other operators in 1928 when the railroad management found that nine out of ten patrons of the park came by auto and bus. Pen Mar Park continued to operate with declining business until gas rationing in 1943 forced it to close.

History of the Appalachian Trail in Maryland

The first trail use along the crest of South Mountain may have been as a route for fugitive slaves making their way north, a link in the Underground Railway. Five of John Brown's men made their way north along South Mountain after the abortive raid on Harpers Ferry. Among John Brown's effects were maps showing mountain forts, and some believe that his strategy may have included building crude forts along South Mountain to cover their retreat after the raid.

A continuous trail along the ridge was not in evidence when the Appalachian Trail was laid out and built across Maryland by members of the PATC. The Trail was marked, cleared and paint-blazed in the winter of 1931 and spring of 1932.

The original five open shelters on South Mountain were constructed in the 1938-41 period. Bear Spring Cabin was dedicated by the PATC on May 1, 1941. Members of the

Mountain Club of Maryland, located in Baltimore, and the Maryland Appalachian Trail Club of Hagerstown assisted members of the PATC in locating sites and negotiating leases with the owners. The Civilian Conservation Corps provided labor and the PATC supplied materials and technical assistance in the construction.

The preservation of the *AT* is now the main problem facing the clubs in this area. Summer homes and other buildings are beginning to encroach on the Trail.

Maryland's Department of Forests and Parks in the mid-1950s announced a plan to acquire land on South Mountain for watershed protection, including the practice of forestry and recreation. By 1964 approximately 4,000 acres had been acquired. The plan lay dormant during the ensuing five years with the exception of the development of the Greenbrier Park. Frederick County, during this period, classified most of the east slope in private ownership in a recreational category that barred new homes for permanent residences but excluded land uses existing at the time of rezoning.

In May 1970, Maryland became the second state to pass legislation to protect the Appalachian Trail. The bill (S.84) directed the state to acquire land for the purpose of protecting and maintaining the Trail across the state. The bill was introduced by State Senator Goodloe Byron of Frederick in January 1970, and was signed by Governor Mandel on May 5, 1970. The *AT* is currently included in South Mountain State Park. Land acquisition, now under Program Open Space of the Department of Natural Resources, is moving ahead.

Although the proposed amendments to the National Trails System Act discussed in Chapter 3 were introduced by two Maryland legislators (Rep. Goodloe E. Byron and Sen. Charles C. Mathias), Maryland does not presently plan to apply for any Federal funds. It expects to complete its purchases solely with state open space funds.

SELECTED REFERENCES

For a complete footnoted version of the preceding history, see the sixth edition. The following publications are among the principal sources:

Dahlgren, Madeline V., *South Mountain Magic* (Boston: James R. Osgood, 1882; Reprinted 1974, Washington Co. Public Library, Hagerstown, Md.).

Maryland Geological Survey, *Report on the Highways of Maryland* (Baltimore: Johns Hopkins University Press, 1889).

Maryland Geological Survey, *Report on the Resurvey of the Maryland-Pennsylvania Boundary* (Baltimore, 1908).

Salzberg, Michael, "Boonsboro Washington Monument," *Washington Post,* March 5, 1970.

Sanderlin, Walter S., *The Great National Project, A History of the Chesapeake and Ohio Canal* (Baltimore: Johns Hopkins University Press, 1946).

Scharf, Thomas J., *A History of Western Maryland* (Philadelphia: Louis H. Everts, 1882).

Schletterbeck, Judy, *The Pen Mar Story* (privately published, 1977).

Williams, Thomas J.C., *A History of Washington County, Maryland* (Hagerstown: Runk and Titsworth, 1906), vol. 1.

Memorial Arch, Gathland State Park

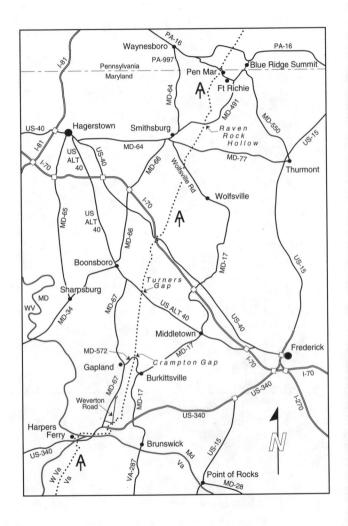

SECTION 1
PEN MAR TO RAVEN ROCK HOLLOW
Distance: 5.8 Miles

Road Approaches and Parking

To reach Pen Mar: From US 15, take Md 550 (Sabillas-
ville Road) west. Turn right at entrance to Ft. Ritchie,
staying on Md 550. Shortly after, turn left and pass under
trestle. A sign at this turn says "Pen Mar Park." Turn right
onto Pen Mar Road. (To reach Pen Mar Park, continue
straight ahead.) Cross into Pennsylvania and over railroad
tracks. The *AT*, going south, follows the powerline right-of-
way on left. There is room for two cars to park on the right
side of the gate here. Do not block gate! Distance is 71 miles
from Washington, D.C.

From I-81, take Md 16 east. Turn right onto Md 418 and
left onto Pen Mar Road. The *AT*, going south, follows the
powerline right-of-way on right just before bridge over
railroad tracks. See above. Distance is 4 miles from Waynesboro.

To reach Raven Rock Hollow: From I-70, take Md 66
north. Turn right onto Md 64 and right onto Md 491 (Raven
Rock Road). *AT*, going north, ascends from stop sign at
intersection with Ritchie Road on left. There is room for four
cars to park on the shoulder of Ritchie Road. Distance is 2.8
miles from Smithsburg.

From US 15, take Md 77 west. Turn right onto Md 64,
then see above.

Points of Interest

Pen Mar Park (at 0.2/5.6 mi) has an outstanding westward view. A former resort, established by the Western
Maryland Railroad, was in operation on this site between
1877 and 1943. Vestiges of former habitation can be seen
just south of the park. High Rock (at 3.2/2.6 mi) offers an

excellent westward view and is a popular site for hang-gliding. Devils Racecourse (0.4 mi down the Devils Racecourse Shelter Trail, at 4.9/0.9 mi) is a remarkable boulder field. Raven Rock, an unusual outcrop, is visible from Md 491 between autumn and spring.

Maps
    PATC Map 5 and USGS Smithsburg Quadrangle

Shelter/Camping
    Devils Racecourse Shelter (0.3 mi down the Devils Racecourse Shelter Trail, at 4.9/0.9 mi) accommodates seven persons and has a *spring* nearby.
    Free camping is allowed just outside Pen Mar Park (at 0.2/5.6 mi). Follow the paved promenade 0.1 mi through the park to High Rock Rd. Camping is permitted in the two fields bounded by High Rock Rd, Chestnut St, Pennsylvania Ave, and Walnut St. Saturday-night campers must leave by 9 a.m. Sunday morning. No public water is available November through April. During these months, it is advisable to call 301-791-3125 during working hours. Camping is *prohibited* except at the above locations. Open fires are allowed only where fireplaces are provided.

Supplies
    Water is available at Pen Mar Park (May through October) and Devils Racecourse Shelter. The park also has a pay telephone.

Brief Description
    The partial ascent of Quirauk Mountain from the north is the most strenuous on the *AT* in Maryland, while from the south is somewhat easier. The main points of interest are concentrated in the northern half of this section.

Side Trails
    High Rock Loop Trail (at 3.1/2.7 mi and 3.2/2.6 mi)
    Devils Racecourse Shelter Trail (at 4.9/0.9 mi)

Detailed Trail Data—North to South

0.0 From Pen Mar Rd pass over *AT* corridor gate and follow *AT* 0.1 mi to start of section at Maryland/Pennsylvania state line (marked by sign on right for "Mason-Dixon Line"). Continuing south on Trail, cross railroad tracks and after 30 yd turn right on ascending grade of former railroad bed.

0.2 Enter grassy area of Pen Mar Park. Continue straight ahead, passing band pavilion on right and dance pavilion on left. Outstanding westward view. From band pavilion path leads through center of park towards parking lot entrance. (To left of central path are rest rooms, unused snack structure, and Visitors Interpretive Center, with pay phone inside. *Water* fountains are on exterior of rest room and snack structures. Park facilities are open May through October, 9 a.m. to sunset. After sunset use portable toilets located beside rest rooms. Hikers may camp on town common, directly outside park entrance.)

0.5 Turn left, climbing embankment, and in 40 yd turn right on old forest road.

0.9 Cross unused forest road (which leads left 0.3 mi to paved High Rock Rd). In 50 yd, 20 ft to right are ruins of stone-lined root cellar; 50 ft to right are ruins of brick-lined, cellar foundation. Many vestiges of former habitation in vicinity.

1.1 Large mound on left, with 3-foot high stone wall on trail side, encloses a deep pit, probably an artificial pond at one time.

1.2 Cross clearing for buried cable. (Clearing leads left 0.12 mi to High Rock Rd.)

1.3 Cross unused forest road which leads left 0.16 mi to gated High Rock Rd.

1.5 Cross unused forest road. (High Rock Rd is 0.15 to left.) Trail becomes very rocky ahead and path is not always obvious. *Follow blazes carefully.*

2.6 Trail passes to right of 40-ft boulder, then between two boulders. In next 0.5 mi Trail ascends 440 ft, crossing several steep rock fields.

3.1 *AT* continues straight where High Rock Loop Trail, blazed blue, enters from left. (Loop Trail leads left 0.1 mi to High Rock, then to parking lot where it turns right, reenters woods and rejoins *AT* at 3.2 mi. High Rock has a spectacular view and is a popular hang-gliding site. Stone foundations and modern cement platform mark site of former 30-ft high pavilion. Paved road, gated dusk to 9 a.m., leads 1.7 mi directly down to Pen Mar Park. Room for 15 cars to park in immediate area of High Rock.)

3.2 Turn right onto old forest road. Blue-blazed High Rock Loop Trail reenters from left.

3.5 Trail continues straight, leaving old road bed where road curves left.

3.9 Local high point and highest elevation on *AT* in Maryland (approx 1890 ft) on southwestern slope of Quirauk Mtn. Begin gentle descent on western slope of South Mountain ridge.

4.6 Beautiful open forest begins. Trail passes a few hemlocks ahead, an unusual growth on a ridge crest.

4.9 Devils Racecourse Shelter Trail, blazed blue, descends 200 ft in 0.3 mi to shelter and *spring.* Unblazed trail beyond shelter leads 0.1 mi to Devils Racecourse, a remarkable boulder field and another 0.1 mi to Ritchie Rd.

5.1 Series of switchbacks for steep descent over next 0.1 mi.

5.4 Clearing on left leads 100 yd downhill to Ritchie Rd.

5.8 Intersection of Ritchie Rd onto Md 491 in Raven Rock Hollow. (Raven Rock, an unusual jutting cliff, is on the north side of Md 491. It can be seen, between autumn and spring, by walking a short distance to the right on Md 491.) To continue on Trail, cross Md 491, bearing 40 yd to right and cross over guard rail.

Detailed Trail Data—South to North

0.0 From the stop sign on Ritchie Rd at intersection of Md 491, *AT* ascends through mixed forest with some hemlocks. (Raven Rock, an unusual jutting cliff, is on north side of Md 491. It can be seen, between autumn and spring, by walking a short distance to the left on Md 491.)

0.4 Clearing on right leads 100 yd downhill to Ritchie Rd.

0.6 Start series of switchbacks for steep ascent over next 0.1 mi.

0.9 Devils Racecourse Shelter Trail, blazed blue, descends 200 ft in 0.3 mi to shelter and spring. (Unblazed trail beyond shelter leads 0.1 mi to Devils Racecourse, a remarkable boulder field, and another 0.1 mi to Ritchie Rd.) Ahead Trail passes through a beautiful open forest containing a few hemlocks, an unusual growth on a ridge crest.

1.7 Open forest ends as undergrowth becomes denser.

1.9 Local high point and highest elevation of *AT* in Maryland (approx 1890 ft) on southwestern slope of Quirauk Mtn.

2.3 Bear left onto old forest road.

2.6 Turn left off old forest road. (Blue-blazed High Rock Loop Trail, straight ahead, leads 0.1 mi to High Rock and rejoins the *AT* at mileage point 2.7 mi. High Rock has a spectacular view and is a popular hang-gliding site. Stone foundations and modern cement platform mark site of former pavilion. Paved road leads 1.7 mi directly down to Pen Mar Park. Road is gated from dusk to 9 a.m. Room for 15 cars to park at High Rock. At parking lot, Loop Trail turns left, reenters woods and descends to mileage point 2.7.)

2.7 High Rock Loop Trail reenters from right. Continue straight. In next 0.5 mi Trail descends 440 ft, crossing several steep rock fields.

3.2 Trail passes between two large boulders and to left of another. Trail becomes very rocky ahead and path is not always obvious. *Follow blazes carefully.*

4.3 Cross unused forest road. (Paved High Rock Rd is 0.15 mi to right.)

4.5 Cross unused forest road which leads right 0.16 mi to gated High Rock Rd.

4.6 Cross clearing for buried cable. (Clearing leads right 0.12 mi to High Rock Rd.)

4.7 Large mound on right, with 3-ft high stone wall on trail side, encloses a deep pit, probably an artificial pond at one time. Many vestiges of former habitation in this vicinity. About 100 yd ahead and 50 ft to left are ruins of brick-lined cellar foundation; 20 ft to left are ruins of root cellar.

4.9 Cross unused forest road which leads 0.3 mi right to High Rock Rd.

5.3 Turn left descending and in 40 yd turn right on old rail bed.

5.5 Enter grassy area of Pen Mar Park. Outstanding westward view. Trail continues straight. (To right of central park path are rest rooms, unused snack structure and Visitors Interpretive Center, with pay phone inside. *Water* fountains are on exterior of rest room and snack structures. Park facilities are open May through October, 9 a.m. to sunset. After sunset use portable toilets located beside rest rooms. Hikers may camp on town common, directly outside park entrance. Parking lot entrance is gated in evening.)

5.6 Exit grassy plateau area of Pen Mar Park, still on old rail bed. About 30 yd beyond gate, near bottom of grade, turn left onto gravel road used by railroad maintenance crews; cross rail line.

5.8 About 50 yd after crossing railroad track, sign on left marks Mason-Dixon Line (now Maryland-Pennsylvania state line) and end of Section 1. In another 0.1 mi Trail crosses Pen Mar Rd. (Pen Mar Park is 0.4 mi to right and Rouzerville, Pa. is 2.0 mi to left.)

Pleasant Valley, Maryland

SECTION 2
RAVEN ROCK HOLLOW
TO WOLFSVILLE ROAD
Distance: 3.5 Miles

Road Approaches and Parking

To reach Raven Rock Hollow: From I-70, take Md 66 north. Turn right onto Md 64 and right onto Md 491 (Raven Rock Road). The *AT*, going south, descends to right, opposite intersection with Ritchie Road. There is room for four cars to park on the shoulder of Ritchie Road. Distance is 2.8 miles from Smithsburg.

From US 15, take Md 77 west. Turn right onto Md 64, then see above.

Warner Gap Road: This gravel road leads one mile east from Md 491 to the *AT*, which crosses the road 0.1 mile after road crosses adjoining stream. There is room for a few cars to park on shoulder at several places between stream crossing and *AT* crossing, *but watch for poison ivy.* Distance is 2.7 miles from Smithsburg.

Foxville Road (Md 77): There is no parking where this road crosses the *AT*. Distances are 2.3 miles west to Smithsburg, 2.7 miles east to Foxville, and 8.7 miles east to Thurmont.

To reach Wolfsville Road (Md 17): From the east, on I-70, take the Myersville exit. Turn right onto Wolfsville Road in the center of Myersville. The *AT*, going north, follows a nameless gravel road, which intersects Md 17 at a point 0.4 mile north of the intersection with Garfield Road and Loy-Wolfe Road. There is room for four cars to park in small gravel lot on south side of Md 17 and for another eight cars along shoulders of gravel road where it joins Md 17. Smithsburg is 2.4 miles northwest, Wolfsville is 3.8 miles south, and Washington, D.C., is 69 miles away.

From the west, on I-70, take Md 66 north. Turn right onto Md 64, then right onto Md 17 and see above.

Points of Interest
   Powerline right-of-way offers a spectacular view (at 2.6/0.9 mi)

Maps
   PATC Map 5 and USGS Smithsburg Quadrangle

Camping
   Camping and open fires are prohibited in this section.

Supplies
   Water is available from *springs* at 0.8/2.7 mi and at 3.4/0.1 mi.

Brief Description
   This section is geographically interesting in that it crosses two small ridges that form a curious, right-angle interruption in the South Mountain range. These ridges extend southeast-ward and link with the Catoctin range. The excellent footing will come as a relief after either adjoining section, but the extremely steep hill at the powerline will be very hard on backpackers going either direction.

Detailed Trail Data—North to South
   0.0 From south side of Md 491, cross guard rail, and 40 yd downhill from intersection of Ritchie Rd descend em-bankment. Cross Little Antietam Creek as it flows down through Raven Rock Hollow.
   0.1 In area dense with hemlocks, pass 8-ft deep hole on right and another similar hole on left in 40 yd. These are probably remnants of 1941 lumbering.
   0.4 Cross 4-ft thick stone wall.

0.5 Reach local high point on east slope of Buzzard Knob. (Abandoned trail on right led to Buzzard Knob which no longer has a view.)

0.8 Turn left onto gravel Warner Gap Rd. In 40 yd turn right, off road. Descend and cross tributary of Little Antietam Creek. *Don't take water from this creek.* In 40 yd a *spring* is beside Trail, under hemlocks on right. Trail ascends steeply for 50 yd.

1.1 Cross old forest road, then bear right where another old forest road enters from left.

1.2 Cross clearing for powerline. No view.

NOTE: A major relocation is being planned for remainder of this section, beginning at 1.3 mi (approx.) and rejoining Trail 0.7 mi into southbound Section 3.

2.0 Pass garage and house on right.

2.2 Bear right onto gravel driveway, passing between trailer on left and house on right. Cross Md 77 (Foxville Rd) and pass through gap in guard rail to right of rod and gun club entrance. Descend very steeply ahead.

2.3 Trail nears top of 30-ft high cliff, then circles right to pass under overhanging rocks of same impressive outcrop.

2.4 Cross polluted tributary of Grove Creek and ascend steeply with rocky footing.

2.6 Leave woods near powerline pylon and turn left. (Spectacular view here to NW.) In 50 yd bear left and begin extremely steep ascent, following natural gas pipeline clearing. At top of hill continue on pipeline clearing to rejoin powerline corridor.

2.9 Bear left to follow near edge of powerline corridor.

3.1 Bear right and cross powerline clearing on old dirt road. Enter woods on opposite side.

3.2 Leave woods to end of private driveway and pass between two garages. Follow driveway.

3.4 Signed side trail leads left 100 yd to stone-enclosed *spring* that provided water to nearby abandoned house.

3.5 Wolfsville Rd (Md 17). To continue on Trail, cross the road.

Detailed Trail Data—South to North

NOTE: A major relocation is being planned, beginning 0.7 mi back in Section 3 and continuing to approximately 2.2 mi into northbound Section 2. Trail crossing at Md 17 will be north of current location.

0.0 From Wolfsville Rd (Md 17), follow nameless gravel road as it descends then ascends. *Stay on road.*

0.1 Signed side trail leads right 100 yd to stone-enclosed *spring* that provided water to nearby abandoned house.

0.3 Pass between two garages for house to left and follow road into woods.

0.4 Cross clearing for powerline, then bear left and follow far edge of clearing.

0.6 Bear right from powerline and ascend hill, now following clearing for natural gas pipeline. At top of hill descend steepest grade of Maryland *AT*.

0.9 At powerline pylon bear right as Trail enters woods. (Spectacular view to NW from pylon clearing.) Descend very steeply with rocky footing.

1.1 Cross polluted tributary of Grove Creek and ascend very steeply.

1.2 Pass under overhanging rocks, then circle to top of impressive outcrop.

1.3 Cross Md 77 (Foxville Road) at entrance to rod and gun club on right. Ascend driveway between house on left and trailer on right. In 50 yd bear left off driveway.

1.5 Pass house and garage on left.

2.3 Cross clearing for powerline. No view.

2.4 Bear left where old forest road continues straight. In 50 yd cross another old forest road.

2.5 Descend very steeply.

2.7 Pass *spring* on left behind hemlocks and ford tributary of Little Antietam Creek. (*Don't take water from creek.*) In 50 yd turn left onto Warner Gap Rd (gravel). In 50 yd turn right off road and ascend into woods.

3.0 Local high point on east slope of Buzzard Knob. Abandoned trail on left led to Buzzard Knob which no longer has view.

3.1 Cross 4-ft thick stone wall. Ahead Trail passes through dense growth of young hemlocks, lumbered in 1941.

3.2 Pass 8-ft deep hole on left and a similar hole on right in 40 yd, probably remnants of the former lumbering operation.

3.5 Cross Little Antietam Creek (flowing through Raven Rock Hollow) and ascend embankment. Cross guard rail to Md 491 in Raven Rock Hollow. To continue on Trail, cross Md 491 and reenter woods near stop sign at intersection of Ritchie Rd.

Black Rock, Maryland

Annapolis Rocks, Maryland

SECTION 3
WOLFSVILLE ROAD
TO INTERSTATE 70
Distance: 8.3 Miles

Road Approaches and Parking

To reach Wolfsville Road (Md 17): From the east, on I-70, take the Myersville exit. Turn right onto Wolfsville Road in the center of Myersville. The *AT*, going south, ascends a gullied road that is opposite a nameless gravel road at a point 0.4 mile north of the junction of Md 17, Garfield Road, and Loy-Wolfe Road. There is room for three cars to park beside Md 17. Smithsburg is 2.4 miles northwest, Wolfsville is 3.8 miles south, and Washington, D.C., is 69 miles away.

From the west, on I-70, take Md 66 north. Turn right onto Md 64, then turn right onto Md 17 and see above.

To reach the Interstate 70 crossing: From the east, on I-70, take Myersville exit. Turn right onto Wolfsville Road (Md 17) in the center of Myersville, then turn left onto US 40. There is room for about 20 cars to park at two pullovers just before US 40 crosses over I-70. From the parking area, cross the embankment and follow the closed section of old highway. At end of old highway, take path around left side of guard rail. Then bear sharply left and descend steeply to footbridge over I-70, on right. (Distance is 0.1 mi from parking.) Turn right onto dirt road between fence and hillside for northbound *AT*, or go straight over footbridge for southbound *AT*. Distance is 60 miles from Washington, D.C.

From the west, on I-70, take the US 40 exit south, just outside of Hagerstown. Cross I-70 overpass and park at pullover on right immediately after. Then see above. Distance is 10 miles from Hagerstown.

Points of Interest

Black Rock Cliffs (at 5.1/3.2 mi) and Annapolis Rocks (0.2 mi down a side trail, at 6.1/2.2 mi) offer outstanding westward views. A talus slope (at 2.2/6.1 mi) offers a good eastward view. The Black Rock Springs Hotel site (at 4.4/3.9 mi) is of historical interest.

Maps

PATC Map 5 and USGS Smithsburg and Myersville Quadrangles

Shelters and Campgrounds

Hemlock Hill Shelter and the surrounding campground (at 0.1/8.2 mi) are privately owned and maintained by Alfred Henneberger, and their use is free on a first-come, first-served basis. It accommodates six persons. There is a *spring* 0.2 mi north on *AT*. Fires are allowed only within the cement fire rings.

Pine Knob Shelter (0.1 mi by side trail, at 7.8/0.5 mi) accommodates five persons and has a *spring* nearby.

The Pogo Memorial Primitive Campsite (at 4.4/3.9 mi) was established by the Mountain Club of Maryland as a memorial to their late member, Walter "Pogo" Rheinheimer, Jr. (1958-1974). Intended for *AT* thru-hikers only, its use is free, on a first-come, first-served basis. The campground has a privy and a nearby *spring*. Camping and open fires are permitted *only* within established fire rings.

Public Accommodations

A restaurant and phone are opposite the entrance to Greenbrier State Park, 0.5 mi west of the US 40 parking area. A bulletin board and display map are at the US 40 parking lot.

Supplies
   Water is available from *springs* near Black Rock Springs Hotel site (at 4.3/4.0 mi), Annapolis Rocks (0.2 mi down side trail, at 6.1/2.2 mi), and Pine Knob Shelter (0.1 mi down side trail, at 7.8/0.5 mi).

Brief Description
   This section presents a typical example of the narrow ridge crest peculiar to Maryland. The Trail follows old roads except for a rough stretch along the crest. The southern half is easier and has the main points of interest. The predominant growth is oak and hickory.

Side Trails
   To Black Rock Cliffs (at 5.1/3.2 mi)
   To Annapolis Rocks (at 6.1/2.2 mi)
   To Pine Knob Shelter (at 7.8/0.5 mi)

Detailed Trail Data—North to South
   0.0 Wolfsville Rd (Md 17). Ascend steeply on old road.
   0.1 Pass Hemlock Hill Shelter on right. (Storms have destroyed most of the hemlocks here. *Spring* is 0.2 mi north on *AT*.) Very steep ascent next 0.1 mi.
   0.2 Begin more gradual ascent to crest of South Mountain.
   0.8 Turn right and in 40 yd reach crest of ridge. In another 40 yd turn left along western slope of South Mountain.
   NOTE: A relocation beginning back in Section 2 will rejoin current AT in this general area.
   1.9 After short, sharp ascent to boulders on left, begin extremely rocky footing as Trail follows eroded crest of South Mountain. There was a small sawmill, just prior to ascent, when this area was lumbered in the 1930s.
   2.2 Good eastward view from talus slope on left.

2.5 Footing improves as Trail becomes slightly undulating old road.

3.4 Continue straight ahead on *AT* where wide, unused forest road ascends right to private land.

3.6 Continue straight ahead on *AT* where forest road descends to left.

3.9 Bear right at junction with old road. (To left, this road descends steeply to junction of Loy-Wolfe Rd and Black Rock Rd in 0.9 mi. This makes possible, on an unblazed route, two circuit hikes using Loy-Wolfe Rd, a very pleasant country road.)

4.2 Two old, unused forest roads intersect *AT* within 50 yd of each other. Bear right at first and left at second.

4.4 Go straight at junction with unused Bagtown Rd (gravel), and enter Pogo Memorial Campsite (privy available) in area of former Black Rock Hotel. Camping on both sides of Trail. (Blue-blazed trail leads 70 yd down gravel road to main *spring*, on right. Smaller *spring* in camp area to right of *AT*. Bagtown Rd descends over 0.9 mi to trailhead parking at end of White Oak Rd, a residential public road off Crystal Falls Rd.)

4.6 Cross intermittent Black Rock Creek and ascend.

5.1 Several unmarked trails lead right 40 yd to Black Rock Cliffs. This 180-degree westward view is the best in this section. Note the considerable scree at the foot of the cliff.

6.1 Blue-blazed trail on right descends sharply 0.2 mi to Annapolis Rocks, an overhanging cliff with an excellent westward view that includes Greenbrier Lake. (Several primitive campsites in immediate area. In campsite area, to left from access spur, blue-blazed trail leads 0.2 mi and 40 ft downhill to *spring* in small draw.)

6.5 Overgrown road intersects on left. Bear right.

7.4 Reach local high point at slight saddle of ridge. (Peak of Pine Knob is to left. Forest road to right leads through private land.) *AT* continues straight, with some very steep descents ahead.

7.7 Blue-blazed trail bearing right leads 0.1 mi to Pine Knob Shelter and *spring*. There are numerous good campsites near shelter.

7.8 Bear left at junction with blue-blazed trail which leads right 0.1 mi to Pine Knob Shelter and *spring*.

7.9 Cross telephone line.

8.1 Pass road leading to farmhouse on left. Then turn right at junction and descend sharply off ridge.

8.2 Pass under US 40 overpass of I-70. Continue ahead on path paralleling I-70 fence line.

8.3 North end of footbridge over I-70 and end of section. (A blue-blazed 0.15 mi spur trail initially continues straight from footbridge. After left turn, then right turn onto old pavement, spur reaches trailhead parking on US 40. Restaurant and phone are 0.5 mi west on US 40.)

Detailed Trail Data—South to North

0.0 From north end of footbridge over I-70, Trail turns left and follows I-70 fence line. (A blue-blazed 0.15 mi spur trail initially continues straight from footbridge. After a left turn, then right turn onto old pavement, spur reaches trailhead parking on US 40. Restaurant and phone are 0.5 mi west on US 40.

0.1 Pass under US 40 overpass for I-70, and ascend into woods.

0.2 Turn left at junction. Just ahead, pass road leading to farmhouse on right.

0.4 Cross telephone line.

0.5 Bear right at junction. (Blue-blazed trail leads left 0.1 mi to Pine Knob Shelter and *spring*. Numerous good campsites near shelter.)

0.6 Continue straight where blue-blazed trail to sharp left leads 0.1 mi to Pine Knob Shelter. Some very steep ascents ahead.

0.9 Reach local high point at slight saddle of ridgeline. (Peak of Pine Knob is to right. Forest road to left leads through private land.) *AT* continues straight, dropping off to east slope of South Mountain.

1.8 Pass overgrown road to right.

2.2 Blue-blazed trail on right descends sharply 0.2 mi to Annapolis Rocks, an overhanging cliff with an excellent westward view that includes Greenbrier Lake. (Several primitive campsites in immediate area. In campsite area, to left from access spur, blue-blazed trail leads 0.2 mi and 40 ft downhill to *spring* in small draw.)

3.2 Several unmarked trails lead 40 yd left to Black Rock Cliffs. This 180-degree westward view is the best in this section. Note the considerable scree at the foot of the cliff.

3.7 Cross intermittent Black Rock Creek.

3.9 Pogo Memorial Campsite (privy available) in area of former Black Rock Hotel. Camping on both sides of Trail. (At north end of campsite unused, gravel Bagtown Rd descends over 0.9 mi to trailhead parking at end of Oak Rd, a residential public road off Crystal Falls Rd. Blue-blazed trail leads 70 yd down gravel road to *spring* on right. In camping area to left of *AT* is smaller *spring* to left.) *AT* continues straight ahead.

4.1 Two unused forest roads intersect *AT* within 50 yd of each other. Bear right at first and left at second.

4.4 Go left at fork. To right, road descends steeply to junction of Loy-Wolfe Rd and Black Rock Rd in 0.9 mi. This makes possible two unblazed circuit hikes using the Loy-Wolfe Rd, a very pleasant country road.

4.6 Continue straight ahead on *AT* where forest road descends to right.

4.9 Continue straight ahead on *AT* where wide but unused forest road ascends left to private land.

5.4 Begin extremely rocky footing as Trail follows sharp, eroded crest of South Mountain.

6.1 Good eastward view from talus slope on right.

6.4 Trail becomes a road again. There was a small sawmill near here when this area was lumbered in 1930s.

7.6 Turn right (overgrown forest road to left) and in 40 yd reach crest of ridge. In another 40 yd turn left and begin descent on eastern slope of South Mountain.

NOTE: A relocation is planned beginning in this general area and rejoining the Trail about 2.2 mi in northbound Section 2.)

8.1 Descend very steeply.

8.2 Pass Hemlock Hill Shelter on left. End of steep descent. (Storms have destroyed most of the hemlocks here. *Spring* is 0.2 mi farther on northbound Trail (see Section 2).

8.3 Wolfsville Road (Md 17). To continue on Trail, cross Md 17 and follow nameless gravel road.

SECTION 4
INTERSTATE 70 TO TURNERS GAP
Distance: 5.0 Miles

Road Approaches and Parking

To reach the I-70 crossing: From the east, on I-70, take the Myersville exit. Turn right onto Wolfsville Road (Md 17) in the center of Myersville, then turn left onto US 40. There is room for about 20 cars to park at two pullovers just before US 40 crosses I-70. From the parking area, cross the embankment and follow the closed section of old highway. At the end of old highway, take path around left side of guard rail. Bear sharply left and descend steeply to footbridge over I-70, on right. Distance is 0.1 mi from parking area; 60 miles from Washington, D.C.

From the west, on I-70, take the US 40 exit south, just outside of Hagerstown. Cross I-70 overpass and park at pullover on right immediately after. Then see above. Distance is 10 miles from Hagerstown.

To reach Turners Gap: From the east, on I-70, take US Alt-40 west. The *AT*, going north, follows Dahlgren Rd on the right at Turners Gap. There is no dependable parking in the vicinity, but the owners of Old South Mountain Inn (0.1 mi west of *AT*) often allow day hikers to park for free, behind the inn, if permission is asked. Distance is 57 miles from Washington, D.C.

From the west, US Alt-40 diverges from US 40 just outside of Hagerstown, but has no junction with I-70. US Alt-40 may also be reached, from I-81, via Md 68; or from Shepherdstown via Md 34. Then see above. Distance is 2 miles from Boonsboro.

From US 340, take Md 67 north and turn right onto US Alt-40. Then see above.

To reach Washington Monument State Park: From US Alt-40 at Turners Gap, turn north onto Washington Monument Rd. Cross Zittlestown Rd and enter park. Entrance and parking are free, but the gate is locked at night. Open 8:00 a.m. to sunset, Friday through Monday all year. Youth group camping may be arranged by lower parking lot.

Points of Interest

The first monument ever erected to George Washington (at 3.0/2.0 mi), in Washington Monument State Park, offers a spectacular westward view. At Turners Gap, the Old South Mountain Inn and Dahlgren Chapel are of historical interest. Also, part of the Battle of South Mountain was fought in the vicinity of Turners Gap.

Maps

PATC Map 5/6, and USGS Myersville and Middletown Quadrangles

Campground

Washington Monument State Park allows camping for youth groups only. Write to Superintendent, Washington Monument State Park, Route 1, Middletown, MD or call 301-432-8065. *Camping and fires are prohibited everywhere else in this section.*

Public Accommodations

Old South Mountain Inn (at Turners Gap) provides dinner 5-9 p.m. Tuesday through Friday; Saturday noon-10 p.m. and Sunday brunch at 10:30 a.m.-2 p.m., regular meals to 8 p.m. No lodging.

Supplies

Boonsboro (2 miles west of Turners Gap) has grocery and hardware stores and a post office.

Water and rest rooms are available at Washington Monument State Park (at 3.2/1.8 mi). There is a public telephone booth at intersection of Washington Monument and Zittlestown roads (3.4/1.6).

Brief Description

This very easy section crosses a succession of low hills almost entirely on forest roads.

Detailed Trail Data—North to South

0.0 Cross footbridge over I-70. Turn left, go up stairs, then turn right and walk on tree-lined Trail easement between two houses. *Stay on Trail.*

0.1 Cross paved Boonsboro Mountain Rd and ascend Bartman Hill on old dirt road. Pass through hickory, oak, maple, dogwood, and sassafras.

0.6 High point on Bartman Hill; begin descent.

0.8 Cross paved Boonsboro Mountain Rd and ascend ahead.

0.9 Cross telephone line.

1.0 Go right at fork off road and onto path.

1.1 Reach local high point and begin descent through lots of laurel, chestnut oak, and American chestnut shoots.

1.4 Cross dirt road and in 150 yd turn left onto another forest road.

1.5 Old road intersects on left. Go straight and ascend.

2.2 Unmarked path leads left short distance to rocks with good winter view. Level, then descend steeply.

2.7 Cross high-tension powerline clearing; ascend Monument Knob very steeply with rocky footing.

2.9 Large talus slope with winter view on right. *Be careful of loose rocks.*

3.0 Intersect graveled path ascending from parking lot; continue straight uphill to first completed monument to George Washington. (First built in 1827, and restored by CCC in 1934-36. See "History Along the Trail." Interior stairs lead to a spectacular view from top of monument. If tower is locked, view from ground level still best view along this section.) Continuing straight, descend very steeply on graveled path ahead.

3.2 Upper parking lot for monument. Museum is first structure to right. Second structure is rest rooms and *water* (in season). Turn left, pass bulletin board, cross entrance road, and enter woods to left of ranger residence.

NOTE: Two relocations are planned: (1) between 3.2 mi to 3.9 mi and (2) between 4.1 to 5.0 mi. (0.1 mi into Section 5)

3.4 Cross entrance road leading right into lower monument parking lot; in 90 yd exit woods to shoulder of Washington Monument Rd. Continue descending and in 70 yd cross Zittlestown Rd (telephone booth on left). Stay with Washington Monument Rd and ascend, passing houses and fields.

3.6 Turn left off road and into maple-dominated woods.

3.9 Cross two stone fences 70 yd apart.

4.0 Path on right leads short distance to small cliff with winter view.

4.1 Local high point; begin descent to Dahlgren Rd.

4.8 Turn right, descending on gravel Dahlgren Rd.

5.0 US Alt-40 at Turners Gap. (To right 0.1 mi is Old South Mountain Inn, used by several Presidents. At least 200 years old, it is one of the oldest public houses along *AT*. Opposite inn is a Gothic stone chapel (open Saturdays, Sundays, and holidays, 1-5 p.m.) built by the widow of Admiral Dahlgren, inventor of the Dahlgren cannon.) To continue on Trail, cross US Alt-40 and pass between guard rail opening.

Detailed Trail Data—South to North

0.0 US Alt-40 at Turners Gap. Ascend graveled Dahlgren Rd. (To left 0.1 mi is Old South Mountain Inn, used by several Presidents. At least 200 years old, it is one of the oldest public houses along *AT*. Opposite inn is a Gothic stone chapel (open Saturdays, Sundays, and holidays, 1-5 p.m.) built by the widow of Admiral Dahlgren, inventor of the Dahlgren cannon.)

NOTE: Two relocations are planned (1) between 0.0 to 0.9 mi, beginning 0.1 mi back in Section 5 and (2) between 1.1 to 1.8 mi.

0.2 Turn left off Dahlgren Rd into woods.

1.0 Path on left leads short distance to small cliff with winter view. Descend.

1.2 Cross two stone fences 70 yd apart.

1.3 Pass through stone fence and descend just ahead through abundant maple.

1.4 Turn right onto paved Washington Monument Rd. Pass houses and open fields ahead.

1.6 Cross Zittlestown Rd (telephone booth on right) and in 70 yd bear left as Trail begins to parallel Washington Monument Rd. In another 90 yd cross entrance road leading into lower monument parking lot.

1.8 Upper parking lot with ranger residence on left. Pass bulletin board, turn right and ascend very steeply on graveled path. (Path beginning at bulletin board is more gradual ascent to monument. Follow edge of parking lot another 80 yd past *AT* to museum and rest rooms. *Water* in season.)

2.0 Pass first completed monument to George Washington and excellent view. (First built in 1827, and restored by CCC in 1934-36. See "History Along the Trail." Interior stairs lead to spectacular view from top of monument.) Continue ahead on graveled path. At curve, go straight, leaving graveled path and descending very steeply.

2.1 Large talus slope left, limited winter view. *Be careful of loose rocks*.

2.3 Cross high-tension powerline clearing.

2.8 Unmarked path leads right short distance to rocks with good winter view. Descend ahead.

3.5 Old road intersects on right. Go straight. Level.

3.6 Go right off road and onto path at fork. Cross dirt road ahead and ascend through lots of laurel, chestnut oaks, and American chestnut shoots.

3.9 Reach local high point and begin descent.

4.0 Bear left onto unused forest road which continues ascending to right.

4.1 Cross telephone line.

4.2 At ridge line gap, cross paved Boonsboro Mountain Rd and ascend Bartman Hill.

4.4 High point on Bartman Hill; descend through hickory, oak, maple, dogwood, and sassafras.

4.9 Cross paved Boonsboro Mountain Rd diagonally to left and follow tree-lined Trail easement between two houses. *Stay on Trail.* Then turn left, descend stairs, turn right, and cross footbridge over I-70.

5.0 North end of footbridge over I-70. To continue on Trail, bear sharp left to parallel I-70. (Blue-blazed trail leads straight from bridge 0.15 mi to large parking lot on US 40.)

SECTION 5
TURNERS GAP TO CRAMPTON GAP
Distance: 7.2 Miles

Road Approaches and Parking

To reach Turners Gap: From the east, on I-70, take US Alt-40 west. The *AT*, going south, follows an old dirt road opposite Dahlgren Rd. There is no dependable parking in the vicinity, but the owners of Old South Mountain Inn (0.1 mi west of *AT*) often allow day hikers to park for free, behind the inn, if permission is asked. (On weekends, park cars in Park, using one car space at the inn for shuttle.) Distance is 57 miles from Washington, D.C.

From the west, US Alt-40 diverges from US 40 just outside of Hagerstown, but has no junction with I-70. US Alt-40 may also be reached, from I-81, via Md 68; or from Shepherdstown via Md 34. Then see above. Distance is 2 miles from Boonsboro.

From US 340, take Md 67 north and turn right onto US Alt-40. Then see above.

Reno Monument Rd: There is no parking at this *AT* crossing.

To reach Crampton Gap: From US Alt-40 (see above), take Md 67 south (from west), or Md 17 south (from east). Then turn onto Gapland Rd (Md 572), which leads to a free parking lot in Gathland State Park at Crampton Gap. Another parking lot at the gap is adjacent to Arnoldtown Rd. Distance is 59 miles from Washington, D.C., and 1.2 miles from the center of Burkittsville.

From US 340, take Md 67 north (from west), or Md 17 north (from east), and see above.

Points of Interest

At Turners Gap, the Old South Mountain Inn and Dahlgren Chapel are of historical interest. Part of the Battle of

South Mountain was fought in the vicinity of Turners Gap, but heavier fighting centered around Fox Gap, where a monument to Major General Reno may be seen (0.2 mi east on Reno Monument Rd, at 1.0/6.2 mi). The small quartzite cliff known as White Rocks at (3.7/3.5 mi) offers a southward view that is poor in summer, but excellent in winter. At Crampton Gap, scene of another Civil War battle, a memorial to Civil War correspondents and the ruins of Gathland may be seen.

Maps
PATC Map 6 and USGS Middletown and Keedysville Quadrangles

Shelters and Campground
Dahlgren Back Pack Campground (at 0.2/7.0 mi), established and maintained by the Maryland Park Service, has numerous excellent sites, rest rooms, *water*, and showers. Use is free on a first-come, first-served basis.

Rocky Run Shelter (0.2 mi by side trail, at 1.9/5.3 mi), first built by the CCC in 1940-41, accommodates five persons. Seasonal *spring*.

Crampton Gap Shelter (0.3 mi by side trail, at 6.8/0.4 mi), first built by the CCC in 1941, accommodates eight persons. *Water* at Park.

Bear Spring Cabin (0.5 mi by side trail, at 4.2/3.0 mi) is a locked cabin owned by the PATC. See "Use of the Guide and the Trail."

Camping is permitted at above camping areas only.

Public Accommodations
Old South Mountain Inn (at Turners Gap) provides meals, but not lodging. (See Section 4: *Public Accommodations*.)

Supplies

Boonsboro (2 mi west of Turners Gap) has grocery and hardware stores and a post office. Burkittsville also has a post office.

Water is available at Dahlgren Back Pack Campground (at 0.2/7.0 mi), from *Bear Spring* (0.3 mi by side trail, at 4.2/3.0 mi), and at Gathland State Park (hand pump beside closed rest room) in season.

Brief Description

This is a relatively easy section with generally excellent footing. The ascent of Lambs Knoll is steeper from the north.

Side Trails

To Rocky Run Shelter (at 1.9/5.3 mi)
White Rocks Trail to Bear Spring Trail (at 3.7/3.5 mi)
Bear Spring Cabin Trail (at 4.2/3.0 mi)
To Crampton Gap Shelter (at 6.8/0.4 mi)

Detailed Trail Data—North to South

0.0 From US Alt-40, opposite junction with Dahlgren Rd in Turners Gap, cross through opening in guard rail and enter woods. In 100 yd turn left onto gravel road providing park ranger access to Dahlgren Back Pack Campground. (To right 150 yd on gravel access road, is gate and parking lot for Old South Mountain Inn, used by several Presidents. At least 200 years old, it is one of the oldest public houses along the *AT*. Opposite the inn is a Gothic stone chapel, open Saturdays, Sundays, and holidays, 1-5 p.m., built by the widow of Admiral Dahlgren, inventor of the Dahlgren cannon.)

NOTE: A relocation is planned which will move the Trail 0.1 mi, to west side of Chapel.

0.1 After 50 yd on access road, turn left as Trail begins to parallel road in woods.

0.2 Pass Dahlgren Back Pack Campground (operated by South Mountain State Park) on right. *Water* (April-Oct), rest rooms, and hot showers. Just ahead, ascend on old road past profuse dogwood.

0.6 Bear right off road and onto path. Descend with rocky footing.

0.7 Cross old trail. Forest ahead is almost entirely chestnut oak.

1.0 Cross paved Reno Monument Rd, west of Fox Gap (originally "Fox's Gap"), which was the scene of heavy fighting during the Battle of South Mountain, Sept. 14, 1862. (The Federal left flank, under Reno, enveloped the Confederate right flank, under Garland, and later under Hood, with the gap as the attack's focal point. Major General Jesse L. Reno and Brigadier General Samuel Garland were killed in the battle, and Rutherford B. Hayes, a future President, was wounded. Reno Monument, erected by veterans of the 9th U.S. Army Corps on Sept 14, 1889, is a steep 0.2 mi to left.)

1.4 Cross high-tension powerline clearing. Excellent westward view.

1.6 Turn right onto old road.

1.9 Blue-blazed trail descends on right 110 ft in 0.2 mi to Rocky Run Shelter and *spring*.

2.4 Bear slightly right and cross paved road. (Paved road is maintenance access to complex of Lambs Knoll communications and FAA towers (to right) and Reno Monument Rd (to left).

3.5 High point near summit of Lambs Knoll. (Unblazed, unmaintained trail to right leads 50 yd to fenced communication tower on summit.)

3.7 *AT* bears right where White Rocks quartzite cliff on left offers a poor summer view, but excellent winter view. In

90 yd on *AT* turn left as trace of closed trail goes right.
(From left side of viewpoint, blue-blazed White Rocks Trail
descends 310 ft over 0.23 mi to intersect Bear Spring Cabin
Trail midway between *AT* and *spring*. This side trail is
rough, steep and not recommended for children. Bear Spring
Cabin Trail then descends another 250 ft over another 0.21
mi to reach *Bear Spring*. Easier access from *AT* at 4.2 mi.)

4.2 Turn right at junction. (Blue-blazed Bear Spring Cabin
Trail descends to left, 360 ft in 0.5 mi, to *Bear Spring* and
another 0.2 mi to PATC locked Bear Spring Cabin. See
chapter on "Side Trails." Highway is 0.35 beyond cabin.)

6.8 Blue-blazed trail leads left 0.25 mi to Crampton Gap
Shelter and intermittent *spring*.

7.1 Reach open field at Gathland State Park, near ruins of
large stone barn (circa 1887) on right. Pass between large
parking lot on left and picnic pavilion on right.

7.2 Pass through gap in stone wall and reach Gapland Rd
(Md 572) at Crampton Gap. (On left, at fork of Arnoldtown
and Gapland rds, is 50 ft tall stone memorial to Civil War
newspaper correspondents, erected by George Alfred
Townsend, a Civil War journalist who used the pen-name
"Gath.") To continue on *AT*, ascend paved driveway to park.
(Museum, Gath Hall and rest rooms for Gathland State Park,
on other side of Md 572, were closed for budgetary reasons
in 1993. *Water* pump to left of rest room structure is
seasonal.)

Detailed Trail Data—South to North

0.0 From Gapland Rd (Md 572) in Gathland State Park,
at Crampton Gap (originally "Crampton's Gap"), pass
through opening in stone wall on north side of Md 572.
Cross field with picnic pavilion on left and parking lot on
right. (The park facilities were closed in 1993. *Water* pump
to left of rest room structure is seasonal. To right are
historical markers and stone memorial to Civil War newspa-

per correspondents, erected by George Alfred Townsend, a Civil War journalist who used the pen-name "Gath." On hill to south is Gath Hall, of the Townsend estate, which was restored as a museum in 1958.) Pass through gap in stone fence and cross field. Heavy fighting occurred here during the Battle of Crampton's Gap, Sept. 14, 1862. (The Federals, under Franklin, eventually overwhelmed the greatly outnumbered Confederates, under McLaws.)

0.1 Pass ruins of large stone barn (circa 1887) and enter woods.

0.4 Blue-blazed trail leads right 0.25 mi to Crampton Gap Shelter and intermittent *spring*.

3.0 As *AT* bears left, blue-blazed Bear Spring Cabin Trail to right descends 360 ft over 0.5 mi to *Bear Spring* and another 160 ft drop and 0.2 mi to PATC locked Bear Spring Cabin. See chapter on "Side Trails."

3.5 Turn right as trace of closed trail continues straight. In another 90 yd, where *AT* bears left, White Rocks quartzite cliff on right offers fair summer view, but an excellent winter view. (Blue-blazed White Rocks Trail descends from left side of rocks (310 ft over 0.23 mi) to intersect Bear Spring Cabin Trail midway between *AT* and *spring*. This side trail is rough, steep and not recommended for children. The Bear Spring Cabin Trail descends another 250 ft over 0.21 mi to Bear Spring Cabin.

3.7 Local high point near summit of Lambs Knoll. (Unblazed, unmaintained trail to left leads 50 yd to fenced, communication tower on summit of hill.)

4.8 Cross paved road, bearing slightly to right. Do NOT take more obvious forest road slightly to left in crossing. (Road, normally gated, is maintenance access to complex of Lambs Knoll communications and FAA towers, to left, from Reno Monument Rd, to right.)

5.3 Blue-blazed trail descends 110 ft over 0.22 mi to Rocky Run Shelter. Ahead *AT* ascends for next 0.3 mi.

5.6 Turn left onto intersecting old road and descend.

5.8 Cross high-tension powerline clearing. Excellent westward view.

6.2 Cross paved Reno Monument Road, west of Fox Gap (originally "Fox's Gap"), which was the scene of heavy fighting during the Battle of South Mountain, Sept. 14, 1862. (The Federal left flank, under Reno, enveloped the Confederate right flank, under Garland, and later under Hood, with the gap as the attack's focal point. Major General Jesse L. Reno and Brigadier General Samuel Garland were killed in the battle, and Rutherford B. Hayes, a future President, was wounded. Reno Monument, erected by the veterans of the 9th U.S. Army Corps on Sept 14, 1889, is a steep 0.2 mi to right.) Rocky footing ahead through forest that is almost entirely chestnut oaks.

6.5 Cross old trail.

6.6 Bear left onto old road and descend through profuse dogwood.

7.0 Pass Dahlgren Back Pack Campground (operated by South Mountain State Park) on left. *Water* (April-Oct), rest rooms, and showers.

7.1 Turn right onto gravel road that provides access to campground. In 50 yd turn right off road onto path. (Access road, in another 150 yd, reaches gate and parking lot for Old South Mountain Inn.)

7.2 US Alt-40 at Turners Gap. (To left 0.1 mi is Old South Mountain Inn, used by several Presidents. At least 200 years old, it is one of the oldest public houses along *AT*. Opposite the inn is a Gothic stone chapel, open Saturdays, Sundays, and holidays, 1-5 p.m., built by the widow of Admiral Dahlgren, inventor of the Dahlgren cannon.) To continue on Trail, cross US Alt-40 and ascend Dahlgren Rd.

SECTION 6
CRAMPTON GAP TO WEVERTON
Distance: 6.7 Miles

Road Approaches and Parking

To reach Crampton Gap: From US Alt-40, take Md 67 south (from west), or Md 17 south (from east). Then turn onto Gapland Road (Md 572), which leads to a free parking lot in Gathland State Park at Crampton Gap. Another parking lot at the gap is adjacent to Arnoldtown Road. Distance is 59 miles from Washington, D.C., and 1.2 miles from the center of Burkittsville.

From US 340, take Md 67 north (from west), or Md 17 north (from east), and see above.

Brownsville Pass Road: On Md 67, park at picnic area beside nameless access road to Brownsville. Overnight parking is not recommended. Hike access road into Brownsville and turn left onto nameless main street of town. Then turn right onto paved road identified by a sign as "Brownsville Pass." This ascends and becomes a dirt road after the last house. Some old blazes are still visible in the woods. Distance from picnic area to Brownsville Gap is about one mile. Distance from Brownsville to Weverton is 4.4 miles.

To reach Weverton: From US 340, take Md 67 north. Then take first right, turning onto "Weverton Rd." This is a 0.2 mi access road to actual Weverton Rd. Midway along road, on right, is *AT* parking area. Trail access is at left side of parking area. Distance is 61 miles from Washington, D.C.

From US Alt-40, follow Md 67 south approx. 12 mi (1.0 mi beyond Garrett Mill Rd on right) and turn onto "Weverton Rd" (last intersection before reaching US 340). Then see above.

Points of Interest
Crampton Gap, scene of heavy fighting during the Civil War, has preserved earthworks, a memorial to Civil War newspaper correspondents, a museum, and the ruins of Gathland. At several places along the ridge, rocky knolls exhibit interesting formations, and numerous beech trees exhibit graffiti (some authentic, some doubtful) from the turn of the century. Weverton Cliffs (0.1 mi by side trail, at 5.8/0.9 mi) offers a magnificent view of the Potomac River gorge.

Maps
PATC Map 6 and USGS Keedysville and Harpers Ferry Quadrangles

Camping
Camping and fires are *prohibited* throughout this section.

Supplies
Water is available only at Crampton Gap, in season. Burkittsville has a grocery store and post office.

Brief Description
The historical interest in Crampton Gap and the view from Weverton Cliffs make this one of the most popular sections of the *AT* in Maryland. The Trail follows both the crest of the narrow ridge and the western rim, with little change in elevation, through a mature forest with excellent footing. North to south is easier because there is a net descent of 570 feet between Crampton Gap and Weverton.

Side trails
To Weverton Cliffs (at 5.8/0.9 mi)

Detailed Trail Data—North to South

0.0 Gapland Road (Md 572) in Crampton Gap, originally "Crampton's Gap." (*AT* parking at large parking area entered from Arnoldtown Rd. On left, at fork of Arnoldtown and Gapland rds, is a 50-ft tall stone memorial to Civil War newspaper correspondents, erected by George Alfred Townsend, a Civil War journalist who used the pen name "Gath.") Pass gate of Gathland State Park and ascend paved driveway. Midway up driveway, on left, is rest room building (closed) but *water* available in season from hand pump at far end, by soda vending machine. (Farther to left is museum for Gathland State Park. At top of driveway, at far end of larger parking lot on right, inside surrounding stone fence line, is Townsend's empty stone mausoleum.) To continue on *AT*, bear left at top of driveway into smaller parking area (serving Gath Hall, to left of *AT*), then continue on gravel path ascending from left rear corner of parking area.

0.1 At slight bend to right, path leads left a short distance to slight remnants of Civil War trenches. (Heavy fighting occurred here during Battle of Crampton's Gap, Sept. 14, 1862. The Federals, under Franklin, eventually overwhelmed greatly outnumbered Confederates, under McLaws.)

1.4 Red granite memorial plaque to Glenn R. Caveney is set flush with ground 10 ft to left of Trail. (Caveney helped maintain this section of Trail with his father. He was killed in an auto accident, and his father established a fund that was used to purchase a 4-acre tract surrounding the memorial, which was dedicated in March, 1976.)

1.8 Cross remains of Brownsville Gap dirt road which, although unblazed, may still be hiked left or right down to adjoining valley highways. Ahead Trail leaves area of Brownsville Gap.

1.9 Cross clearing for buried communication cable.

3.1 Blue-blazed trail leads 100 ft right to mediocre winter view of Pleasant Valley and Elk Ridge.

3.7 Turn left onto old road at junction.

3.8 Giant beech on right has oldest graffiti dates ("1892" and "1899") that have been found on beeches on this ridge.

4.7 Old road intersects on right. Go straight.

5.8 Blue-blazed trail on left, at right bend in Trail, leads 0.1 mi to Weverton Cliffs. (This magnificent view of Potomac River gorge should not be missed.) Ahead Trail continues descent using 16 well-engineered switchbacks. (Set in stone at the cliffs, 20 ft to right of Trail, is a plaque in memory of Congressman Goodloe E. Byron, 1928-78, a great supporter of the *AT*.)

6.7 Cross Weverton Rd and in 80 yd follow left side of intersecting public road, along edge of lawn. Section ends adjacent to left side of *AT* parking lot on Weverton (access) Rd. (Md 67 is 0.2 mi farther along public road.) To continue on Trail, bear left as Trail skirts small field behind parking area then crosses same field.

Detailed Trail—South to North

0.0 From left side of parking lot, follow 20-ft access path to *AT*. Parallel public highway at foot of embankment, then cross lawn of private yard. Cross Weverton Rd. Beside a telephone pole enter woods and begin 480-ft ascent via 16 well-engineered switchbacks to spur leading to Weverton Cliffs.

0.9 Blue-blazed trail on right leads 0.1 mi to Weverton Cliffs. (This magnificent view of the Potomac River gorge should not be missed. Set in stone at the cliffs, 20 ft to left of Trail, is a plaque to the memory of Congressman Goodloe E. Byron, 1928-78, a great supporter of the *AT*.)

2.2 Go right at fork.

2.8 Giant beech on left has oldest graffiti dates ("1892" and "1899") that have been found on beeches on this ridge.

3.0 Turn right onto intersecting old road.

3.6 Blue-blazed trail leads 100 ft left to mediocre winter view of Pleasant Valley and Elk Ridge.

4.9 Cross clearing for buried communication cable. Ahead, go right then left at forks as Trail nears Brownsville Gap Rd.

5.0 Cross remains of Brownsville Gap dirt road which, although unblazed, may still be hiked left or right down to adjoining valley highways.

5.3 Red granite memorial plaque to Glenn R. Caveney is set flush with ground 10 feet to right of Trail. (Caveney helped maintain this section of Trail with his father. He was killed in an auto accident, and his father established a fund that was used to purchase a 4-acre tract surrounding the memorial, which was dedicated in March 1976.)

6.6 Path to right leads a short distance to slight remnants of Civil War trenches. (Heavy fighting occurred here during the Battle of Crampton's Gap, Sept. 14, 1862. The Federals, under Franklin, eventually overwhelmed the greatly outnumbered Confederates, under McLaws.) Ahead, enter smaller of two paved parking lots for George Townsend's Gath Hall, the stone house to right. Follow paved driveway down to public highway. (At far end of larger parking lot on left, inside surrounding stone fence line, is Townsend's empty stone mausoleum.) Midway down driveway, on right, is rest room building, closed, but *water* available in season at hand pump at far end (by soda vending machine. (Farther to right is museum for Gathland State Park. Museum, Gath Hall and rest rooms were closed in 1993 for budgetary reasons.)

6.7 Gapland Rd (Md 572) at Crampton Gap. (On right, at fork of Arnoldtown and Gapland rds, is a 50-ft tall stone memorial to Civil War newspaper correspondents, erected by George Alfred Townsend, a Civil War journalist who used the pen-name "Gath.") To continue on Trail, cross Md 572 and pass through gap in stone fence.

SECTION 7
WEVERTON TO HARPERS FERRY
Distance: 3.3 Miles

Road Approaches and Parking

To reach *AT* parking lot at Weverton: From US 340, take Md 67 north, then take first right onto "Weverton Rd." This is a 0.2 mi access road to actual Weverton Rd. Midway along road, on right is *AT* parking area. Trail access is at left side of parking area. Distance is 61 miles from Washington, D.C.

From US Alt-40 take Md 67 south, approx. 12 miles (1 mile beyond Garrett Mill Rd on right.) Turn left onto Weverton Rd (last intersection before reaching US 340).

To reach Harpers Ferry: From US 340, turn onto Shenandoah St (the "entrance" road for Harpers Ferry National Historical Park), at west end of bridge over Shenandoah River. Free parking, inadvisable overnight, in small lot on corner of Shenandoah St and US 340. For additional parking, at $5 per car, stay on US 340 and proceed to Harpers Ferry NPS Visitor Center. Park and take tour bus back to historic area of Harpers Ferry. Continue to end of Shenandoah St, turn right, and pass under trestle. The *AT*, going north, crosses the Potomac River on the Goodloe Byron Memorial Footbridge, on left. Distance is 61 miles from Washington, D.C.

To reach Keep Tryst Rd and Sandy Hook Rd: From US 340, turn onto Keep Tryst Road. Continue straight to reach parking along road, located at 0.4/2.9 mi in Trail section. Harpers Ferry Hostel and additional parking may be reached by turning right from Keep Tryst Rd onto Sandy Hook Rd (known as Harpers Ferry Road inside the park boundary). Hostel is on left at sharp curve in road. Three parking areas are located beside road beyond railroad trestle; access to *AT* at Goodloe Byron Memorial Footbridge is 0.4 mi southeast along Chesapeake and Ohio Canal towpath.

Points of Interest
The Chesapeake & Ohio Canal is of historical interest, and the Goodloe Byron Memorial Footbridge offers a superb view of the Potomac River.

Maps
PATC Map 6 and USGS Harpers Ferry Quadrangle

Campgrounds
Weverton Primitive Camp (100 yd by side trail, at 0.8/2.5 mi), by the Potomac, has *no privy* and *no water* (the river is polluted), but is the only place where free camping is possible in this section. There is camping space in the yard of the Hostel (see below).

Public Accommodations
Harpers Ferry Hostel, operated by the Potomac Area Council of the American Youth Hostel, has a 39-bed capacity (0.4 mi by side trail, at 2.0/1.3 mi; see Loudoun Heights Trail, in chapter on "Side Trails," for directions). It is open from 5 p.m. to 9:30 a.m., Mar 15-Nov 15. Hostel is equipped with bunks, toilets, towels and showers, cooking and laundry facilities, and a phone, but does not provide meals. The per-night fees are $11 for members of AYH, ATC, or PATC; $14 for non-members. Camping in the large yard costs $6 for members, $9 for non-members. (Children are half-price.) *Reservations* may be made using a credit card; *payment* must be made with *cash or check*.

Supplies
There is a grocery store in Sandy Hook (70 yd by side trail at 2.0/1.3 mi). A motel and restaurant are near the

Maryland end of the US 340 bridge (Sandy Hook Bridge) over Potomac River.

Water and a telephone are available at the Hostel (see above).

Brief Description

For most of this section, the Trail utilizes the towpath along the abandoned the Chesapeake & Ohio Canal, a National Historical Park. The level terrain and excellent footing make this the easiest section in this book. The scenery, with the Potomac River on one side and the canal on the other, offers a pleasant change from the adjoining ridges.

Side Trails

To Weverton Primitive Camp (at 0.8/2.5 mi)
Loudoun Heights Trail (at 2.0/1.3 mi)

Detailed Trail Data—North to South

0.0 From left side of *AT* parking lot follow 20-ft access path to *AT*. At Trail turn right and in 50 yd right again to cross short overgrown field. Ahead *be careful of precipitous drop* to Israel Creek, on right.

0.2 Cross under US 340 overpass. A dirt "road" and pilings of a former bridge may be seen along Israel Creek. These mark the route of the former Washington County Railroad, which later became the Hagerstown Branch of the Baltimore & Ohio Railroad.

0.4 Reach inside radius of hairpin turn in Keep Tryst Rd. (Toadflax flowers may be seen here.) Continue straight (past informal parking area) to NPS gate on outside radius of road. Bear right and cross CSX (formerly Baltimore & Ohio) Railroad tracks.

0.5 Cross causeway over abandoned Chesapeake & Ohio Canal and turn right onto towpath. (The 184.5 mile canal, which linked Washington and Cumberland, was completed in 1850. Operation ended in 1924, after the canal was severely damaged by a storm. The canal is now a National Historical Park.) Trail blazes will be found occasionally on posts along the towpath.

0.8 Blue-blazed trail leads 100 yd left to Weverton Primitive Camp. *No water*; the river is polluted. Ahead, pass a few private houses and several paths to the Potomac River.

2.0 Cross under Sandy Hook Bridge and continue on towpath. On right, blue-blazed Loudoun Heights Trail leads 3.2 mi, via Sandy Hook (US 340) Bridge, to rejoin the *AT* in Virginia Section 1. It passes a grocery store in Sandy Hook and the Harpers Ferry Hostel. (See chapter on "Side Trails.")

2.7 Pass canal lock on right.

3.1 Pass under the first of two trestles, turn left, and ascend metal stairs of Goodloe Byron Memorial Footbridge, which crosses the Potomac River. (Congressman Goodloe E. Byron, 1928-78, was a great supporter of the *AT*.) Hikers wishing to reach the Grant Conway Trail should continue on the towpath. (See chapter on "Side Trails.")

3.3 Bulletin board at end of brick walkway in Harpers Ferry. An adjacent post bears map of *AT* route through town. Overlook on left has superb view of Potomac and Shenandoah confluence. To continue on the Trail, turn right and pass under trestle.

Detailed Trail Data—South to North

0.0 Bulletin board at beginning of brick walkway. Follow walkway to Goodloe Byron Memorial Footbridge and cross Potomac River. (Congressman Goodloe E. Byron, 1928-78, was a great supporter of the *AT*.) Overlook on right has superb view of Potomac and Shenandoah confluence.

0.2 Turn right onto Chesapeake & Ohio Canal towpath. (The 184.5 mile canal, which linked Washington and

Cumberland, was completed in 1850. Operation ended in 1924, after the canal was severely damaged by a storm. The canal is now a National Historical Park.) Hikers wishing to reach Grant Conway Trail should turn left onto towpath at this junction. (See chapter on "Side Trails.") Trail blazes will be found occasionally on posts along towpath.

0.6 Pass canal lock on left.

1.3 On left, blue-blazed Loudoun Heights Trail leads 3.2 mi, via Sandy Hook (US 340) Bridge to rejoin *AT* in Virginia Section 1. It passes a grocery store in Sandy Hook and Harpers Ferry Hostel. (See chapter on "Side Trails.") Cross under Sandy Hook (US 340) Bridge and continue on towpath.

2.5 Blue-blazed trail leads 100 yd right to Weverton Primitive Camp. *No water;* the river is polluted.

2.8 Turn left off towpath and onto dirt road used by NPS ground maintenance crews. Cross over canal, cross CSX (formerly Baltimore & Ohio) Railroad tracks and bear left to NPS gate at outside radius of sharp turn in Keep Tryst Rd. (Toadflax flowers may be seen here.) *AT* enters woods at inside radius of turn.

3.1 Cross under US 340 overpass. (A dirt "road" and pilings of a former bridge may be seen along Israel Creek, the deep ravine on the left. These mark the route of the former Washington County Railroad, which later became the Hagerstown Branch of the Baltimore & Ohio Railroad.) Ahead, *be careful of precipitous drop* on left, then cross overgrown field and turn left.

3.3 Reach 20-ft spur connecting *AT* parking area on south side of Weverton "access" Rd. To continue on Trail, bear right and parallel public highway at foot of embankment.

CHAPTER 6
HARPERS FERRY

GENERAL INFORMATION

Harpers Ferry is one of the outstanding historical and scenic attractions on the *AT*. It became a National Historical Park in 1963. From north to south, the Trail passes through the scene of John Brown's raid, and then makes its way along the slope of a cliff, past the famous Jefferson Rock.

Two key *AT* offices are located in Harpers Ferry: (1) the headquarters of the Appalachian Trail Conference, and (2) the Appalachian Trail Project Office of the National Park Service.

HISTORY

Peter Stephens, a trader, settled in Harpers Ferry (then called "The Hole") in 1733 and established ferries across both rivers. Robert Harper purchased "squatter's rights" from Stephens and purchased the land, in 1747, from the legal holder, Lord Fairfax. The following spring, Fairfax engaged Peter Jefferson (father of Thomas) to survey the land. The survey party included fifteen-year-old George Washington, who later revisited this area several times before designating Harpers Ferry as the site for a national arsenal in 1796.

Beginning in the late 1700s, water transportation was improved with bypass canals around the rapids of the two rivers. The C&O Canal along the Potomac to Georgetown (Washington, D.C.) began operations from Harpers Ferry in the early 1830s, providing access to Tidewater markets. Early in the nineteenth century, Harpers Ferry became an important transportation and industrial center, attracting a produce center, hotels, saloons, and livery stables to service the town. The water-level gateway through the mountains also attracted the B&O Railroad which soon gave the C&O Canal strong competition, and eventually won out. Here, the Winchester and Potomac Railroad (which became a branch of the B&O) joined the main line. Today, the towpath of the canal is "a natural" for a hiking trail. The towpath, across the Potomac from the town, leads downriver approximately 61 miles to Washington and upriver 124 to Cumberland.

An interesting historical and nature hike of 1.5 miles is found on Virginius Island. One of the National Park Service publications available at the Visitor Center provides a key to the numbered stakes along the trail and describes the natural and historical features. Here was the site of an industrial village: a cotton textile mill with gas lighting, sawmill, flour mill, iron foundry, rolling mill, carriage factory, rifle factory (which introduced the system of interchangeable parts), and row houses. The entire industrial complex depended on water power, the source for industrial energy in the early 1800s; the underground culverts that carried the intricate system of raceways may be traced. Devastated by flood, fire, and war, the area now approximates the natural conditions when the white man arrived. The rich verdure on the alluvial deposits now covers all but scattered vestiges of human improvements.

Harpers Ferry never recovered from the John Brown raid in 1859 and the following Civil War. (The Brown raid and the role of Harpers Ferry in the Civil War are adequately covered in the free leaflet available at the Visitor Center.) In addition to war, fire, flood, and pestilence (cholera and typhoid epidemics) ravaged the town. Technological advancements in power no longer made it necessary to locate factories at the water's edge where floods were a recurring threat.

Most of the town lay in ruins when the Harpers Ferry National Monument (a designation of the National Park

Service) was provided for in a congressional enabling act of 1944. The first land was acquired in 1952, and the Harpers Ferry National Historical Park was created in 1963. In addition to the downtown facilities and Virginius Island, land extending to Loudoun Heights across the Shenandoah, Bolivar Heights, and Elk Ridge to a point beyond the Stone Fort in Maryland, have been added. The State of Virginia has not exercised its right by the 1944 Congressional enactment to provide land for the park.

POINTS OF INTEREST

Buildings in downtown Harpers Ferry have been restored to the 1859-65 era. Currently, buildings and interior exhibits are open from 8 a.m. to 6 p.m. daily. The Visitor Center is located in the Stagecoach Inn (1826). A slide program and exhibits tell the history of Harpers Ferry and the story of John Brown's raid. (Rest rooms are located in the building adjacent to the Visitor Center.) The Master Armorer's House, down Shenandoah Street from the Visitor Center, contains an exhibit on gun making.

The fire engine house where Brown and his men made their last stand was located across Potomac Street on the site marked by a stone obelisk. The original building was removed from Harpers Ferry for a financially unsuccessful venture at the Columbian Exposition in Chicago in 1893. The present replica is slightly smaller than the original; many of the original bricks were taken for souvenirs during the periods when it was dismantled.

Store windows along Shenandoah Street display merchandise of a century ago, as well as tools and artifacts unearthed in the restoration and archaeological excavations. Foundations of the arsenal and a trench showing destroyed muskets are visible. The foundations of some of the rectangular armory buildings may be seen on the Potomac River side of the town in a neglected sunken garden adjacent to the relocated railroad station.

The *AT* passes the last house of Robert Harper. Built between 1775 and 1781, it is the oldest surviving structure in town. It was restored by the Park Service and furnished with period pieces by the Women's Clubs of the county. The building is open daily.

The *AT* also passes Jefferson Rock, which is on a bluff overlooking the Shenandoah and the gap across to Loudoun Heights. The present Jefferson Rock is a flat stone supported by red sandstone pillars rising from a larger rock at the edge of the cliff.

The original rock associated with Jefferson was a balanced one. Captain Henry, a Federalist stationed at Harpers Ferry, and men of his company, stirred by Jefferson's campaign promise to reduce appropriations for defense in 1800, pried the large boulder loose and sent it crashing to the quarry below. Jefferson described the views in his "Notes on Virginia" in 1782:

> You stand on a very high point....On your right comes up the Shenandoah....On your left approaches the Potomac, in quest of a passage also. In the moment of their junction, they rush together against the mountain, render it asunder, and pass off to the sea....For the mountain being cloven asunder, she presents to your eye, through the cleft, a small catch of smooth blue horizon, at an infinite distance of the plain country....This scene is worth a voyage across the Atlantic. Yet here, as in the neighborhood of the Natural Bridge, are people who have passed their lives within a half a dozen miles, and have never been to survey these monuments of a war between rivers and mountains....

Later, when Thomas Jefferson was President, he remembered an eagles' nest in a large oak seen from this vantage point and requested the Superintendent of the Arsenal to procure some eagles. Nailing slats on the trunk of the tree, the son of the Superintendent and two friends climbed the tree and captured three eaglets. Jefferson sent one of the young eagles to the King of Spain, who in turn gave the President an Andalusian ram. The early White House lawn mower delighted in chasing boys who teased him. The ram with the spreading horns was successful in one of his pursuits and the impact killed a young man by the name of Carr. The President sold the ram and thus Andalusian sheep were first introduced into this country.

The view of the merging of the two rivers from the present Jefferson Rock is partially obscured by buildings and trees. From a point where the two rivers merge, the spire of Chimney Rock may be discerned one-third of the way up Loudoun Heights.

For further information on the area, the Visitor Center on Shenandoah Street is recommended. Reference material in the form of books and magazine articles concerning Harpers Ferry are numerous.

REFERENCES

Joseph Barry, *The Strange Story of Harpers Ferry* (The Shepherdstown Register, W.Va., 1958).

E. L. Bowen, *Rambles in the Path of the Steam Horse* (Philadelphia: Wm. Brownell and Wm. White Smith, 1854).

Philip S. Forner, *Basic Writings of Thomas Jefferson* (New York: Wiley, 1944).

Harpers Ferry, West Virginia

CHAPTER 7
NORTHERN VIRGINIA AND WEST VIRGINIA

GENERAL INFORMATION
Distance: 58.0 Miles

This segment of the *AT* begins at the southern end of the Goodloe Byron Memorial Footbridge in Harpers Ferry. For about 14 miles after leaving Harpers Ferry it follows the ridge crest that forms the boundary between Virginia and West Virginia. It zigzags across the state line, with its total mileage in West Virginia (including Harpers Ferry) somewhat over 7 miles.

After a steep climb from the bridge over the Shenandoah River to the crest, the Trail follows the narrow crest of the Blue Ridge south past ruined stone breastworks of the Civil War period, through a section frequently burned over. This was the first section of Trail that the PATC constructed, in 1927-28. Some of this area is now included in the Harpers Ferry National Historical Park.

On each side of Snickers Gap, the *AT* skirts a long-established summer community. From Crescent Rock to Ashby Gap, land closings have forced the Trail off the main ridge and onto a route that crosses a succession of side ridges and hollows. Within this section, the *AT* passes Mt. Weather, a classified government installation operated by the Federal Emergency Management Agency.

For similar reasons, the Trail snakes along the slopes on each side of the Blue Ridge from Ashby Gap to Manassas Gap. The relocation of the Trail in these two sections represents one of the PATC's foremost successes in Trail protection.

South of Manassas Gap, the Trail climbs, east of Linden, over an abandoned, mountaintop farm with fine views and passes over the slopes of High Knob before descending to the west of Chester Gap. Then the Trail passes through the woods and fields of Harmony Hollow, on the western side of the Blue Ridge, to Shenandoah National Park.

From north to south, the Blue Ridge changes from a narrow ridge to a wider expanse of side ridges and outlying mountains. This is accompanied by an increase in the variety of growth that can be seen along the Trail.

The Trail in this chapter has been divided into the following sections:

HISTORY ALONG THE TRAIL

The first part of the Appalachian Trail to be established between the Hudson Valley and the Great Smokies was opened south of Harpers Ferry in 1927 by the newly formed Potomac Appalachian Trail Club. Within two years, a handful of members had made the Trail a reality as far as Rockfish Gap. Their work inspired the formation of other groups, which completed other links in the 2,000-mile footpath.

The PATC appointed its first Trail overseer in this region. Within two years of its opening, the original section of Trail was nearly lost because of fire, undergrowth and neglect. Walter R. Jex was assigned to maintain the *AT* from Harpers Ferry to Bluemont, a distance of 18 miles. Other PATC members soon took responsibility for other Trail sections, and the system of Trail overseers was born.

Early History

History in the conventional sense has happened only in bits and pieces along the Trail south of Harpers Ferry, while to the west in the Shenandoah Valley it has occurred on the grand scale. The natural barrier of the Blue Ridge has helped to channel settlement, commerce, and even war into the great flow of history up and down the valley. Along the Trail, however, we speak more of men crossing the ridge on missions of importance to the lands below.

Before the coming of the white man, this region was sparsely settled by tribes of the Powhatan Confederation to the east and by the Shawnees to the west. Other tribes, mentioned in the Maryland section of this *Guide*, used two great trails for war and migration. East of the ridge, in Loudoun and Fauquier counties, lay the Great War Road. To the west, in the Shenandoah Valley, was the major Indian trail that later became the chief route for white men as well; that trail is now known locally as the Valley Pike and more generally as US 11.

The first explorer to cross the Blue Ridge was a German, John Lederer, who made three successive trips to the Blue Ridge in March and May of 1669 and in August of 1670. On this last trip he discovered the northern pass into the Shenandoah Valley, probably Chester Gap, since he ascended the Rappahannock. The monument commemorating his discovery is located at Manassas Gap, however, just off the *AT* at Linden, Va. In 1707, the French explorer Louis Michelle led a party from Maryland into the Shenandoah Valley at Harpers Ferry and traveled as far south as Massanutten Mountain.

Settlement in the Blue Ridge began in the 1720s when German immigrants moved south from Pennsylvania, taking up land in the middle section of the Shenandoah Valley. The lower valley was not fully settled until after the French and

Indian War, when Virginia planters moved in from the Tidewater.

The Appalachian Trail in northern Virginia and West Virginia lies within the original grant of Charles II to the Lords Fairfax, which conveyed all lands between the Potomac and Rappahannock rivers. Much was sold for settlement (and some taken by squatters), but in 1736 Thomas Lord Fairfax ordered a 120,000-acre tract surveyed, which he established as his Manor of Leeds. This included the entire Blue Ridge from Snickers Gap to Chester Gap and much of the Shenandoah Valley adjacent to it. When Fairfax settled in Virginia in 1748, he built his manor house, Greenway Court, near White Post. His surveyor that year was a 16-year-old lad named George Washington.

The Manor of Leeds was subsequently divided into lesser manors, all of which figured in speculation during the region's first land boom. A syndicate, consisting of John Marshall, James Marshall, and their brother-in-law Raleigh Colston, acquired the Manor in 1793. A clouded title prevented them from selling land, however, nearly bringing financial ruin until the courts cleared the title in 1806.

Blue Ridge Gaps

Five gaps in the Blue Ridge have always provided the essential contacts in northern Virginia between the Piedmont and the Shenandoah Valley. Known by various names in the past, they are now called Keys Gap, Snickers Gap, Ashby Gap, Manassas Gap, and Chester Gap.

Keys Gap, formerly Vestal's Gap, was served by a ferry on the Shenandoah as early as 1747, where at that time the region had its first iron industry. Washington used this route in 1754 during the campaign to Great Meadows and Fort Necessity, as did part of Braddock's army in 1755. (The name has variously been spelled Keys and Keyes; in February 1964, however, the Board of Geographic Names of the U.S. Geological Survey decided on Keys.)

Snickers Gap was named for Edward Snicker, who operated a ferry across the Shenandoah before 1764. It was originally known as Williams Gap, but has had its present name through most of its history. Snicker's name did not stick to the ferry, however, which became known as Castleman's. Washington used this route in his later years when he visited his cousin at Berryville and his brothers at Charles Town.

Ashby Gap was originally called the Upper Thoroughfare of the Blue Ridge and was served at the Shenandoah by Berry's Ferry. The main road to the valley, the Winchester Pike, passed through the gap, and it was along this route that Washington traveled on his first trip to the valley in 1748. Cornwallis's captured troops were marched through the gap to Winchester in 1781.

Ashby Gap received its present name from the Indian fighter, Colonel John Ashby, whose family settled near what is now Paris. The name also brings to mind his noted descendent General Turner Ashby, Confederate cavalry leader under General Stonewall Jackson.

Manassas Gap (Manassa's Gap, according to a probably apocryphal legend) was at one time known as Calmes Gap, after Marquis Calmes, a colonial figure whose name also appears on a bend of the Shenandoah River known as Calmes Neck.

Chester Gap once went by the name Happy Creek Gap.

Railroad Development

These gaps naturally attracted considerable interest during the railroad building era, especially after the B&O preempted the Potomac water-level route at Harpers Ferry. Because of its low elevation, Manassas Gap was the most attractive, and by 1854 a railroad by that name ran from its junction with the Orange and Alexandria Railroad at Manassas through the gap to Strasburg in the Shenandoah Valley.

One other railroad scheme involved both Keys Gap and Snickers Gap. This is remembered by many area residents as the Washington & Old Dominion Railroad, which served Bluemont from 1900 to 1939. The railroad originated in the 1840s as the Alexandria, Loudoun & Hampshire Railroad, which was to reach Winchester by way of Vestal's (Keys) Gap. Financial troubles dogged the line, and it had only reached the Catoctin Ridge by the Civil War. After a change of name to Washington, Ohio & Western (WOW), a change in route to Snickers Gap, and receivership, the rails finally came to Snickersville in 1900. That same year the town adopted a more euphonious name, Bluemont.

Construction of the railroad to Bluemont may have influenced the building of many turn-of-the-century summer homes in the Bluemont area. This early development made it difficult to locate a route for the Appalachian Trail when it was later established.

Civil War Action

The Blue Ridge figured prominently in many Civil War actions. Jackson marched his troops through Ashby Gap on July 18, 1861, before the First Battle of Bull Run. They bivouacked at Paris before boarding the Manassas Gap Railroad to reach the battle just in time.

A year later, in September 1862, Confederate troops under Jackson's command climbed Loudoun Heights to bombard Harpers Ferry and forced its surrender with 11,000 Union troops just before the Battle of Antietam. Also on Loudoun Heights, the Confederate raider, Colonel John S. Mosby, attempted to overrun a sleeping encampment of Maryland cavalry on January 10, 1864. He was discovered before he could spring the attack and was repulsed by half-dressed Union soldiers after a sharp fight that resulted in four deaths on each side.

To the south, Snickers Gap witnessed the retreat of General Jubal Early in July 1864, after his raid on Washington, D.C. In this gap in November 1864, Union troops laid an ambush for John Mobley, a former Mosby follower who led his own band to harass Union forces around Harpers Ferry. His death was largely due to information received after a $1,000 reward was put on his head.

The entire region from Snickers Gap to Manassas Gap and east to the Bull Run Mountains was under the influence of Colonel Mosby, the "gray ghost," and soon earned the name of "Mosby's Confederacy." Mosby's men lived in farmhouses throughout the region and gathered on command for their operations. Paris and Linden were frequent rendezvous sites.

South of Ashby Gap is Signal Knob, one of several promontories in the region used regularly for communications by both sides during the Civil War.

Scientific Activities

After the war, the most notable developments on the Blue Ridge occurred near Snickers Gap and brought science to the forefront. In October 1868, near Bears Den Rocks, Dr. Mahlon Loomis conducted one of the most significant but unrecognized experiments of the time, whereby he nearly discovered the existence of radio waves and operated the first radio antenna. He and a colleague on Catoctin Ridge, 18 miles away, simultaneously raised kites with copper gauze attached, on a copper wire, which was attached to a galvanometer. In a prearranged sequence, the two men attached one or the other galvanometer to ground wires and secured readings on the opposite instrument. Loomis thought of electricity as being like an ocean with a force that resembled waves of ripples; his purpose was to develop a form of aerial telegraph. This experiment took place 20 years before Hertz demonstrated the existence of radio waves.

In 1900 Professor Willis L. Moore, Chief of the U.S. Weather Bureau, proposed bringing together on the Blue Ridge a number of advanced weather research activities. Thus, in 1901, Mount Weather began operation with the eventual goal of investigating terrestrial magnetism, thermodynamics of the atmosphere, solar-physical and upper air phenomena, and model weather research. Work did not get underway uniformly on all projects, but early in 1907 the Mount Weather Station achieved the highest ascent of a kite in history (five miles). This ascent provided invaluable instrument recordings on the upper atmosphere. After 1907, however, the Mount Weather project languished, and occasional proposals were offered to revive the facility for various purposes. One such was to make it a summer White House during the Coolidge administration. In recent years, Mount Weather has been developed as a classified government installation, and is closed to public entry.

West of the Appalachian Trail in Chester Gap lies another government installation with an interesting past. It was originally acquired by the U.S. Army in 1911 as a remount station to provide a supply of horses and mules. Later it served as a prisoner-of-war camp, and was also used for training K-9 dogs. Its usefulness to the Army diminished after the war, and in 1948 the property was transferred to the U.S. Department of Agriculture, which used it as a beef cattle research station and conference center. These operations were discontinued in the early 1970s, and the facility and land were transferred to the National Zoological Park (for a Research and Conservation Center) and to Virginia Polytechnic Institute (for a 4-H center).

Trail Route Status

Although the *AT* route in northern Virginia and West Virginia was one of the earliest parts of the Trail, this does not mean that the route is well established. From the start, relatively little was on public property. Some private property owners have, over the years, been increasingly reluctant to have the Trail cross their property. Where a key piece of property is involved, long sections of Trail have been effectively blocked.

In the last few years, the National Park Service land acquisition program has protected a permanent, woodland route for nearly the entire northern Virginia and West Virginia stretch. This protection effort was aided by key purchases by the PATC in the early stages, and by the cooperation of the state of Virginia.

WEST VIRGINIA HISTORY

In 1863 West Virginia became a state, and Jefferson County, Virginia, became a part of the new state. Along the state line the Appalachian Trail meanders back and forth using the best geographical features of the top of the Blue Ridge. (For information on Harpers Ferry, see Chapter 6.)

SELECTED REFERENCES

Davis, Julia, *The Shenandoah* (New York: Rinehart, 1945).

Harwood, Herbert H. Jr., *Rails to the Blue Ridge* (Falls Church, Va.: Pioneer American Society, 1969).

Leighton, Marion, "Mosby's Confederacy," *PATC Bulletin,* January 1939.

Loudoun County Civil War Centennial Commission, *Loudoun County and the Civil War: A History and Guide* (Leesburg, Va., 1961).

Schairer, Frank, "Early Days of the Appalachian Trail," *PATC Bulletin*, July-September 1969.

Solyom, Herbert L., "Mount Weather," *PATC Bulletin,* January 1941.

Strain, Paula, "Kite String Antenna," *PATC Bulletin,* December 1968.

Wayland, John W., *Twenty-five Chapters on the Shenandoah Valley* (Strasburg, Va.: Shenandoah Publishing House, 1957).

Wellman, Manley Wade, *Harpers Ferry, Prize of War,* (Charlotte, NC: McNally, 1960).

Weverton Cliffs, Maryland

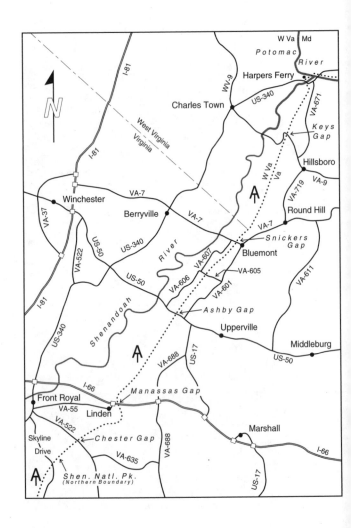

SECTION 1
HARPERS FERRY TO KEYS GAP
Distance: 6.3 Miles

Road Approaches and Parking

To reach Harpers Ferry: From US 340, turn onto Shenandoah St (the "entrance" road for Harpers Ferry National Historical Park) at west end of bridge over Shenandoah River. Free parking, inadvisable overnight, in small lot on corner of Shenandoah St and US 340. For additional parking, at $5 per car, stay on US 340 and proceed to Harpers Ferry NPS Visitor Center. Park and take tour bus to historic area of Harpers Ferry. Then continue on Shenandoah St to intersection with High St, the first street on left. The *AT*, going south from the opposite direction, turns here onto High St. Distance is 61 miles from Washington, D.C.

Keys Gap: This is on WVa 9. The *AT* crosses the highway a few yards from the state line. A parking area for about 12 cars lies beside the Trail, on the northern side of the highway. Hillsboro, Va., is 6 miles east; Charles Town, W. Va., is 7.4 miles west. It is about 52 miles from Washington, D.C.

Points of Interest

There is an excellent viewpoint at Jefferson Rock (at 0.2/6.0 mi). Several rock redoubts, built as Civil War defenses for Harpers Ferry, may be seen beside the Trail between 2.3/3.9 mi and 2.6/3.7 mi. For additional points of interest, see Chapter 6: Harpers Ferry.

Maps

PATC Map 7 and USGS Harpers Ferry and Charles Town Quadrangles

Camping

Camping and fires are prohibited in the Park.

Public Accommodations and Supplies

Harpers Ferry has a hotel, post office, and various stores and services. Detailed information can be obtained at ATC headquarters, on corner of Washington and Jackson streets.

Stores with food and *water* lie 0.3 mi either side of *AT* at Keys Gap. Eastern store has pay phone and rest rooms.

Brief Description

This is a relatively easy section, especially for northbound hikers, who face a net descent of about 600 feet. The footing is good except for a rough 1.3 mi segment.

Side Trails

To ATC headquarters (at 0.7/5.6 mi)
To viewpoint (at 2.1/4.2 mi)
Loudoun Heights Trail (at 2.4/3.9 mi)

Detailed Trail Data—North to South

0.0 Bulletin board at end of brick walkway. An adjacent post bears map of *AT* route through town. (The Trail and streets are unmarked between here and the cliff, due to park regulations.) Turn right and pass under trestle ahead. (Overlook on left has superb view of Potomac and Shenandoah confluence.) Then turn left onto Shenandoah St, the first street past the trestle. (On left is replica of fire engine house in which John Brown made his stand. Old Federal arsenal foundations are adjacent.) Go one block on Shenandoah St, passing building with "John Brown Story" sign.

0.1 Turn right onto High St. (The Park Visitor Center is straight ahead on Shenandoah St.) Turn left past first house on left and ascend very steep stairway. (To reach ATC headquarters and a post office, continue on High St (becomes

Washington St) about 0.5 mi to its intersection with Jackson St. ATC is on the left corner. A post office is two blocks farther.) Ahead, pass "Armory Workers' Apartments" on right and continue straight up road, passing Robert Harper's house (1775-81, the town's oldest) on right corner and St. Peter's Roman Catholic Church (1833) on left.

0.2 Go straight up stairs, leaving road where road bears to right, and pass ruins of St. John's Episcopal Church (1852) on right. Seventy yards ahead, go right at fork by "Harper Cemetery" sign. (Left path leads a few yards to excellent view from Jefferson Rock.)

0.3 Go straight at cross-paths. (Path on right leads a few yards to Harpers Cemetery.) Ahead, the Trail undulates along the cliff. *Watch for poison ivy.*

0.4 Go straight. (Path on right leads to Storer College campus.) Stay on cliff and ignore intersecting paths ahead.

0.7 Blue-blazed trail leads 0.2 mi right to ATC headquarters. Go straight. Ahead, go right at fork.

1.0 Descend cliff to junction of US 340 and Shenandoah St. Follow narrow pedestrian walk across bridge over Shenandoah River.

1.3 End of bridge. Cross to right side of US 340 and ascend stairs on cliff. Splendid winter view ahead.

1.4 Cross ravine filled with hemlocks.

1.6 Cross ravine and ascend through beautiful, profuse growth of periwinkle.

1.7 Cross WVa 32.

1.8 Turn left. Trail parallels old gullied road.

1.9 Trail crosses gullied road. Ahead, ascend very steeply at times, with occasional switchbacks.

2.1 Turn right at junction. (To left, path leads to side trail shown on map, no longer open.)

2.2 Turn right onto old road.

2.3 Turn left, off road and onto path, where bulldozed mounds of earth block road.

2.4 Ridge crest. Turn right at junction. On left, blue-blazed Loudoun Heights Trail leads 3.2 mi to rejoin the *AT* in Maryland Section 7. (See chapter on "Side Trails.") Ahead, leave Harpers Ferry National Historical Park and pass rock redoubts dating from the Civil War. (When Lee invaded Maryland in 1862, he detailed Jackson to capture Harpers Ferry, which fell after a short siege, Sep. 13-15. Brigadier General John G. Walker's division bombarded the town from these heights. The redoubts were infantry defenses built and abandoned by the Federals.)

3.1 Ascend steeply.

3.4 Level, with rocky footing ahead.

4.2 Possible campsite on left. Descend.

4.7 Cross high-tension powerline clearing. Go straight at crossroad in center of corridor. View of Short Hill Mtn. to east, but western view is almost entirely blocked by summer growth. Footing is good again.

5.0 Ascend slightly, then level. Rocky footing in places ahead. Continue to ascend and descend.

5.9 Old road intersects on right. Go straight.

6.1 Bear left at two successive forks. Ahead, barbed-wire fence and old field on left. *Watch for poison ivy.*

6.3 Pass bulletin board with *AT* information and parking lot on right and reach WVa 9. To continue on Trail, cross WVa 9.

Detailed Trail Data—South to North

0.0 WVa 9. Pass bulletin board with *AT* information and parking lot on left.

0.1 Barbed-wire fence and old field on right. *Watch for poison ivy.*

0.2 Fence ends. Go straight as two successive trails intersect on left.

0.4 Go right at fork. Ascend ahead and descend.

0.7 Level, then descend slightly. Rocky footing in places ahead.

1.3 Ascend. Good footing.

1.6 Cross high-tension powerline clearing. Go straight at crossroad in center of corridor. View of Short Hill Mtn. to east, but western view is almost entirely blocked by summer growth. Rocky footing ahead.

2.1 Possible campsite on right. Level.

2.9 Footing becomes good again. Descend steeply.

3.2 Ascend.

3.7 Ahead, pass several rock redoubts dating from the Civil War. (When Lee invaded Maryland in 1862, he detailed Jackson to capture Harpers Ferry, which fell after a short siege, Sept 13-15. Brigadier General John G. Walker's division bombarded the town from these heights. The redoubts were infantry defenses built and abandoned by the Federals.)

3.9 Enter Harpers Ferry National Historical Park. *Camping and fires are prohibited*. Then turn left and descend. (Straight ahead, blue-blazed Loudoun Heights Trail leads 3.2 mi to rejoin the *AT* in Maryland Section 7. See chapter on "Side Trails.")

4.0 Turn right onto old road, near bulldozed mounds of earth.

4.1 Turn left off road and onto path.

4.2 Turn left and descend very steeply at times, with occasional switchbacks. (Straight ahead, path leads to side trail shown on map. This trail is no longer open.)

4.4 Trail crosses old gullied road. Descend less steeply.

4.5 Turn right, away from road.

4.6 Cross WVa 32 and descend on path through beautiful, profuse growth of periwinkle.

4.7 Cross ravine.

4.9 Cross ravine filled with hemlocks. Splendid winter view from cliff ahead.

5.0 Turn left onto US 340 and cross bridge over Shenandoah River via narrow pedestrian walk.

5.3 Cross to right side of US 340 at junction of US 340 and Shenandoah St (the Park "entrance" road) in Harpers Ferry. Ascend cliff very steeply. *Watch for poison ivy.* (The Trail and streets are unmarked through the town, due to Park regulations.)

5.6 Blue-blazed trail leads 0.2 mi left to ATC headquarters. Go straight. Trail undulates ahead. Stay on cliff and ignore intersecting paths.

5.9 Go right at fork. (Path on left leads to Storer College campus.)

6.0 Go straight at cross paths. (Path on left leads a few yards to Harper Cemetery.) Descend, sometimes steeply. Ahead, path on right leads a few yards to excellent view from Jefferson Rock.

6.1 Pass ruins of St. John's Episcopal Church (1852) on left, descend stairs, go straight onto paved road, and pass St. Peter's Roman Catholic Church (1833) on right. Where road bears to left, go straight down stairs, passing Robert Harper's house (1775-81, the town's oldest) and "Armory Workers' Apartments," both on left. At bottom of stairs, turn right onto Washington St (becomes High St).

6.2 Turn left onto Shenandoah St. (The Park Visitor Center is to right.) After one block, turn right and pass under trestle. (On right is replica of fire engine house in which John Brown made his stand. Old Federal arsenal foundations are adjacent.)

6.3 Turn left at bulletin board at beginning of brick walkway. (Straight ahead, overlook has superb view of Potomac and Shenandoah confluence.) To continue on the Trail, follow brick walkway to Goodloe Byron Memorial Footbridge.

SECTION 2
KEYS GAP TO SNICKERS GAP
Distance: 13.5 Miles

Road Approaches and Parking

Keys Gap: This is on Va 9. The *AT* crosses the highway on the West Virginia side of the state line. A parking area for about 12 cars lies beside the Trail, on the northern side of the highway. Hillsboro, Va., is 6 miles east; Charles Town, W. Va., is 7.4 miles west. It is about 52 miles from Washington, D.C.

To reach Blackburn Trail Center: From Va 7 or Va 9, take Va 719. Turn onto Va 713 and follow it almost to the top of the ridge, avoiding all private driveways.

Snickers Gap: This is on Va 7. The *AT* crosses Va 7 slightly west of the gap. Numerous cars can park on the southwest corner of Va 7 and Va 601. Several cars can park where the *AT* leaves Va 679. From Snickers Gap, Bluemont is 1.8 miles east, and Washington, D.C., is about 52 miles east.

Points of Interest

There are views from Buzzard Rocks (at 3.6/9.9 mi), from an outcrop (at 6.1/7.4 mi), from Crescent Rock (at 10.9/2.6 mi), which also has unusual rock formations, and from two outcrops (at 11.8/1.7 mi and 12.9/0.6 mi). Other points of geological interest are The Lookout (at 6.8/6.6 mi) and Devils Racecourse (at 10.3/3.1 mi). The misnamed Laurel Swamp (at 5.2/8.2 mi) has a beautiful growth of periwinkle and a former house site.

Maps

PATC Map 7 and USGS Charles Town, Round Hill, and Bluemont Quadrangles

Shelters and Campgrounds

David Lesser Shelter (115 yd by side trail, at 3.0/10.5 mi) has a deck with bench and accommodates 6 persons under the roof. Facilities include covered picnic table, fireplace, and privy. *Spring* is quarter mile down hill.

Blackburn Center Campground (0.1 mi by side trail, at 6.2/7.3 mi), owned and maintained by the PATC, has a privy, fire ring, grill, and picnic table. Use is free on a first-come, first-served basis. *Water* is available at the Blackburn Center.

Blackburn Trail Center (0.3 mi by side trail, at 6.4/7.0 mi) is a house and two outbuildings owned and maintained by the PATC as a work center and recreation site. Club members are often present. Posted Trail information, logbook, a pay phone, and *water* are available within the screened, but unlocked, porch. The Center's Hodgson House, a primitive cabin (beds and wood stove only), sleeps eight; open all year free to *AT* thru-hikers.

Public Accommodations

Pine Grove Restaurant lies 0.9 mi north of *AT* on Va 679. Closed Sunday afternoons and Mondays.

Supplies

Stores with food and *water* lie 0.3 mi either side of *AT* at Keys Gap. Eastern store has pay phone and rest rooms.

Water and telephone are available at Blackburn Center (0.3 mi by side trail, at 6.4/7.0 mi).

Water is also available from *Sand Spring* (70 yd on side trail, at 10.3/3.1 mi), and sometimes from the intermittent *Laurel Spring* at (5.3/8.2 mi).

There is a post office in Bluemont, which has a General Delivery mail-drop that can be used by hikers.

A grocery store at Snickers Gap lies 1.0 mi north of *AT* on Va 679.

Brief Description
    This section, mostly along the ridge crest, offers an interesting hike with considerable variety. The length, numerous undulations, and occasional rocky footing make it one of the most rugged sections in this book. It is a moderately difficult day hike.

Side Trails
    To David Lesser Shelter (at 3.0/10.5 mi)
    To Buzzard Rocks (at 3.6/9.9 mi)
    To Blackburn Center and Campground (at 6.2/7.3 mi and 6.4/7.0 mi)
    To *Sand Spring* (at 10.3/3.1 mi)
    To Crescent Rock (at 10.9/2.5 mi)
    To *spring* (at 11.2/2.2 mi)

Detailed Trail Data—North to South
    0.0 WVa 9 in Keys Gap. *AT* turns right and angles away from highway, passing through field. *Watch for poison ivy.* Ahead, old *AT* route intersects on right; go straight.
    0.1 Cross polluted stream flowing from pond. Several paths in open woods make Trail hard to follow. *Watch for blazes.* Trail goes straight, then curves to left just ahead and generally ascends soon thereafter.
    1.6 Go left at fork and ascend. In 50 yd go right at fork.
    1.7 Cross old road. Ascend, sometimes steeply.
    2.0 Turn right onto old road at junction, then go left at fork just ahead.
    2.1 Winter view to east. Ahead, descend through a young forest on western side of crest.
    3.0 Blue-blazed trail leads left 115 yd to David Lesser Shelter. (*Spring* and overflow campsite 0.2 mi farther downhill.) *AT* continues straight as forest road changes into rocky path for short, very steep ascent up small knoll before descending again.

3.2 Slight eastward view. Just ahead, pass what appears to be a small remnant of a chimney, a few yards to right.

3.3 Ascend steeply.

3.6 Blue-blazed trail leads right 0.1 mi to Buzzard Rocks. (Path forks. Right branch leads to scree with no view. Left branch leads to Buzzard Rocks, with limited summer view of Shenandoah River and Shannondale Lake. Good site for one tent near view.) *AT* descends very steeply over boulder ahead, then more moderately.

3.7 Ascend generally with rocky footing.

4.1 Level. The Deer Lick, a mossy area not visible from the Trail, is on left a short distance before this point.

4.2 Descend.

4.5 Bear left onto old Shannondale Rd (which intersects as a path on the right), then turn right off road just ahead. (The road once connected Hillsboro to Shannondale Springs, a famous 19th-century resort that was patronized by Presidents.)

4.9 Ascend along eastern side of ridge crest.

5.1 Descend.

5.2 The misnamed "Laurel Swamp." Beautiful, profuse growth of periwinkle covers former house site on right. Rock walls outline yard, and slight chimney ruins are visible. Garden terraces rise above the site.

5.3 Path leads right a few yards to walled-in *Laurel Spring*, which is often dry. Ascend.

6.1 Quartzite cliff on right offers good view.

6.2 Blue-blazed trail on left descends very steeply to campground (left fork in 0.1 mi) and to Blackburn Trail Center, in 0.3 mi. *Water* is available (not dependable in winter) from Blackburn Center. An easier route to the Center is 0.2 mi ahead. Descend generally ahead.

6.4 Blue-blazed trail on left leads to Blackburn Trail Center in 0.3 mi.

6.8 Pass The Lookout, an unusual pile of boulders on left. This once offered a fine eastward view, hence the name, but trees have now completely blocked the view.

6.9 Come into old road. (Short distance to right, road ends at clearing with good view.)

7.2 Path leads right to winter view from rocks. Descend steeply.

7.4 Go right, off road and onto path, at fork in Wilson Gap. Road ahead is posted "No Trespassing." *This is easy to miss.*

NOTE: A relocation is planned between Wilson Gap and Sand Spring.

7.6 Cross very gullied old road. Ascend steeply.

8.1 Reach ridge crest.

8.6 Descend with rocky footing.

8.8 Ascend very steeply with rocky knoll on right.

8.9 Level. Winter view from rocky crest on left.

9.2 Ascend.

9.6 Except for one small rise, the Trail ahead descends a side ridge with rocky footing.

10.2 Cross telephone line and turn right onto old road. On left, paralleling the road, is Devils Racecourse, a boulder field with a small stream running beneath it, similar to its namesake in Maryland Section 1.

10.3 Turn left off road, cross Devils Racecourse and ascend steeply ahead. (Straight ahead, road leads to *Sand Spring*, on right, in 70 yd.)

10.6 Go right at fork and descend through red maple, chestnut oak, sassafras, laurel, dogwood, and chestnut shoots.

10.9 Crescent Rock. Excellent view of the Shenandoah River and Valley. The distinctive sloping terminus of Massanutten Mountain can be seen in the distance. (From Crescent Rock, a path leads west along cliff about 100 feet to point where cliff can be descended. By walking back, along base of cliff, to foot of Crescent Rock, one can see the geological fold that forms a crescent in the rock. The core of the fold has been broken out by the action of ice in the crevices, forming a six-foot deep, arch-shaped indentation in the cliff. Pulpit Rock, or the "pinnacle," stands about 150 feet west of Crescent Rock. It is a column of rock that is separated from the cliff by a gap of about 10 feet. *The danger of snakes makes it inadvisable to descend the cliff during warm weather.)* Ahead, begin very steep, 500-foot descent. *Slippery at all times.*

11.2 Go left at fork. Blue-blazed trail on right leads 50 yd to *spring*, passes a less desirable *spring*, and rejoins *AT* after 100 yd.

11.3 Blue-blazed trail rejoins on right. Go straight. Norway maples here. In a few more feet, go right at fork, cross rocky creek bed, and ascend steeply through yellow poplars.

11.4 Bear right and ascend very steeply at first, then more easily, on rocky hillside. *Watch for poison ivy.*

11.7 Level. Descend ahead.

11.8 Good view of Shenandoah Valley from quartzite outcrop on right. Descend very steeply through black tupelo (blackgum), laurel, azaleas, and pine.

12.2 Level. Young oaks, older pines.

12.4 Begin general descent.

12.6 Go straight at crossing with path. Descend steeply.

12.7 Cross stream in Pigeon Hollow. Ahead, ascend gradually, then very steeply at times, by long switchbacks through rocks.

12.9 Fine view of Valley from rock outcrop. Trail undulates ahead, sometimes steeply.

13.4 Turn left onto Va 679.

13.5 Post with *AT* sign in median strip of Va 7, slightly west of Snickers Gap. (Bluemont is 1.8 mi east.) To continue on Trail, turn left and follow Va 7 east.

Detailed Trail Data—South to North

0.0 Post with *AT* sign in median strip of Va 7, slightly west of Snickers Gap. Follow Va 679 north. In 50 yd, turn right off road and ascend steeply into woods. Trail undulates ahead, sometimes steeply, through laurel, pine, and chestnut oak.

0.6 Fine view of Shenandoah Valley from rock outcrop. Descend ahead, sometimes steeply, by long switchbacks through rocks.

0.8 Cross stream in Pigeon Hollow. Ascend steeply. Ahead, go straight at crossing with path.

1.1 Level. Young oaks, older pines.

1.3 Ascend gradually at first, then very steeply, through laurel, azaleas, pine, and black tupelo (blackgum).

1.7 Good view of Shenandoah Valley from quartzite outcrop on left.

1.8 Descend gradually at first, then very steeply through rocks. *Watch for poison ivy.*

2.1 Bear left and descend steeply through yellow poplar forest.

2.2 Bear left and cross rocky creek bed; pass path that intersects on right, and then bear right at fork. Blue-blazed trail on left leads past a poor *spring*, to a better *spring* in 50 yd and rejoins *AT* after 100 yd. Norway maples here. Ahead, blue-blazed trail rejoins *AT* on left. Begin 500-ft ascent gradually at first, then very steeply. *Slippery at all times.*

2.6 Crescent Rock. Excellent view of the Shenandoah River and Valley. The distinctive sloping terminus of Massanutten Mountain can be seen in the distance. (From Crescent Rock, a path leads west along the cliff about 100 feet to a point where the cliff can be descended. Then by walking back, along the base of the cliff, to the foot of Crescent Rock, one can see the geological fold that forms a crescent in the rock. The core of the fold has been broken out by the action of ice in the crevices, forming a six-foot deep, arch-shaped indentation in the cliff. Pulpit Rock, or the "pinnacle," stands about 150 feet west of Crescent Rock. It is a column of rock that is separated from the cliff by a gap of about 10 feet. (*The danger of snakes makes it inadvisable to descend the cliff during warm weather.*) Ascend through red maple, dogwood, laurel, and oak.

2.8 Bear left at junction with old road. Descend steeply ahead.

3.1 Cross Devils Racecourse, a boulder field with a small stream running beneath it, similar to its namesake in Maryland Section 1.

3.2 Turn right onto old road and ascend. (To left, road leads to *Sand Spring* in 70 yd.)

NOTE: A relocation is planned between Sand Spring and Wilson Gap.

3.3 Turn left, off road and onto path, cross telephone line, and ascend steeply with rocky footing.

3.9 Descend, rejoining main ridge.

4.3 Level. Ahead, winter view from rocky crest.

4.6 Descend very steeply with rocky knoll on left.

4.7 Ascend.

4.8 Reach ridge crest.

5.4 Descend steeply.

5.9 Cross gullied old road and ascend steeply.

6.0 Bear left onto road in Wilson Gap. To right, road is posted "No Trespassing."

6.3 Path leads left to winter view from rocks. Ascend more gradually ahead.

6.6 Continue straight, leaving road. (Short distance to left, road ends at clearing with good view.) Ahead, pass The Lookout, an unusual pile of boulders on right. This once offered a view, hence the name, but trees have now completely blocked view.

7.0 Blue-blazed trail on right descends steeply 0.3 mi to Blackburn Trail Center. *Water* is available (not dependable in winter) from the Center.

7.3 Blue-blazed trail on right descends very steeply to campground (left fork in 0.1 mi) and to Blackburn Center, in 0.3 mi.

7.4 Quartzite cliff on left offers good view.

8.1 The misnamed "Laurel Swamp." Path leads left to walled-in *Laurel Spring*, which is often dry.

8.2 Beautiful, profuse growth of periwinkle covers former house site on left. Rock walls outline yard, and slight chimney ruins are visible. Garden terraces rise above the site. Ascend.

8.3 Descend along eastern side of ridge crest.

8.6 Ascend.

8.9 Turn left onto old Shannondale Rd, then turn right off road just ahead. (The road once connected Hillsboro to Shannondale Springs, a famous 19th-century resort that was patronized by Presidents.)

9.2 Level.

9.4 Descend generally, with rocky footing. Just ahead, on right, is The Deer Lick, a mossy area not visible from the Trail.

9.8 Ascend steeply.

9.9 Blue-blazed trail leads left 0.1 mi to Buzzard Rocks. (Path forks. Right branch leads to scree with no view. Left branch leads to Buzzard Rocks, with limited summer view of Shenandoah River and Shannondale Lake. Good site for one tent near view.) Descend steeply.

10.1 Ascend.

10.3 Pass what appears to be a small remnant of a chimney, a few yards to left. Slight eastward view just ahead.

10.5 After short, rocky, very steep, descent, blue-blazed trail leads right 115 yd to David Lesser Shelter. (*Spring* and overflow campsite 0.2 mi farther donwhill.) *AT* continues straight, ascending by old forest road to western side of ridge crest.

11.3 Winter view to east. Descend steeply ahead.

11.4 Bear right onto old road, then go left at fork just ahead. Descend ahead, sometimes steeply.

11.8 Cross old road.

11.9 Pass intersecting old road on right. In 50 yd pass intersecting old road on left. Generally level ahead.

12.4 Descend generally.

13.4 Trail becomes level in open woods with several paths. *Watch for blazes*. Trail crosses polluted stream flowing from pond, then goes right at fork with old *AT* route and crosses field.

13.5 WVa 9 in Keys Gap. (Stores with food and *water* lie 0.3 mi either side of *AT*. Eastern store has pay phone and rest rooms.) To continue on Trail, cross WVa 9.

SECTION 3
SNICKERS GAP TO ASHBY GAP
Distance: 14.1 Miles

Road Approaches and Parking

Snickers Gap: This is on Va 7. The *AT* crosses Va 7, 0.25 mi west of the gap. Numerous cars can park in lot used by carpool participants on the southwest corner of Va 7 and Va 601. Limited parking on northeast corner of Va 7 and Va 679. From Snickers Gap, Bluemont is 1.8 miles east, and Washington, D.C., is about 52 miles east.

To reach Va 605: Take Va 601 south from Snickers Gap, or north from Ashby Gap, and turn onto Va 605, a driveable dirt road, at Mt. Weather. There is room for a couple of cars to park on the powerline right-of-way, at the *AT* crossing, about 1.4 miles west of Va 601.

Ashby Gap: This is on US 50. The *AT* crosses US 50 0.25 mi west of the gap. PATC has a 10-car parking lot on the west side of Va 601, about 0.2 mile north of Va 7. A blue-blazed access trail at the back of the lot descends to the *AT* in 85 yd (at 13.9/0.2 mi). Paris is 1.0 mile east, and Washington, D.C., is 56 miles east.

Points of Interest

There are excellent views from Bears Den Rocks (at 0.6/13.5 mi), Lookout Point (at 3.0/11.1 mi) and Buzzard Hill (at 5.0/9.1 mi). The dark and cool Fent Wiley Hollow (at 4.63/9.5 mi) has a great variety of mature timber. The Trail also passes a former cabin site (at 5.5/8.6 mi).

Maps

PATC Map 8 and USGS Bluemont and Paris Quadrangles

Shelters

Sam Moore Shelter (0.1 mi by side trail, at 3.6/10.5 mi) accommodates six persons. It stands next to *Sawmill Spring* and has a privy, fireplace, and sheltered picnic table.

Rod Hollow Shelter (0.1 mi by side trail, at 10.5/3.6 mi) accommodates seven persons. It has a *spring*, privy, and sheltered picnic table and hearth.

Public Accommodations

Pine Grove Restaurant lies 0.9 mi north of Va 7 on Va 679. Closed Sunday afternoons and Mondays.

Horseshoe Curve Restaurant is 0.3 mi north of Va 7 on Va 679. Open Tues-Sat, noon-10 p.m.; Sun noon-6 p.m.

Bears Den Hostel (0.2 mi by side trail, at 0.6/13.5 mi) has 20 bunks, toilets, showers, washer, dryer, cooking facilities, and telephone. No food is provided, but the hostel does sell soft drinks and snacks. The hostel is closed from 9:30 a.m. to 5:00 p.m. (road is gated). Check-in is from 5-9 p.m. A "day-use" room and showers are available during the day for hikers only. Nightly fees per person are $12 for members of AYH, ATC, or PATC; $15 for others; $6.00 for camping in yard (with use of facilities). Hikers may take *water* during the day from a tap on the left side of the house entrance, but must be sure to *turn it off*.

Indian Trading Post is on US 50 just to east of Trail in Ashby Gap. Snacks only. Phone booth.

Blue Ridge Restaurant is 0.8 mi west on US 50.

Supplies

The hostel and restaurants (see above) have telephones.

The Village Market grocery store at Snickers Gap lies 1.0 mile north of Va 7 on Va 679.

Water is available at the Bears Den Hostel (see above), and from *springs* at 0.9/13.2 mi, at 3.6/10.5 mi (intermittent), at 5.6/8.5 mi, and at Rod Hollow Shelter at 10.5/3.6 mi.

Brief Description

Land closings have forced the *AT* off the main ridge in this section, but the Trail now follows a stable route on a protected corridor to the west. Consequently, the Trail seesaws in and out of a succession of hollows and over numerous side ridges, making this probably the most difficult section in this book. (*Poison ivy* may be a problem in some areas.) Nevertheless, the route may be seen as an interesting contrast to the ridge-walking that dominates most of the *AT* route in Maryland and northern Virginia.

Side Trails

To Bears Den Hostel (at 0.6/13.5 mi)
To *spring* (at 0.9/13.2 mi)
To Sam Moore Shelter (at 3.6/10.5 mi)
To Rod Hollow Shelter (at 10.5/3.6 mi)
To Myron Glaser Cabin (at 12.3/1.8 mi)
To parking lot on Va 601 (at 13.9/0.2 mi)

Detailed Trail Data—North to South

0.0 Section begins at median strip on Va 7, 0.25 mi west of Snickers Gap, at junction of Va 679. Go east on south shoulder of Va 7. (Bluemont is 1.8 mi east of the gap.)

0.1 Turn right off Va 7 and onto graveled driveway, which narrows to a path almost immediately. Ascend generally, through dogwood, yellow poplar, oak, laurel, and sassafras.

0.6 Bears Den Rocks on right has outstanding view of Shenandoah Valley. Path on left leads 0.2 mi to Bears Den Hostel (*tap water* available).

0.7 A path on left leads 0.2 mi to Hostel.

0.9 Blue-blazed trail on left leads 125 yd to *spring*.

1.2 Cross creek on footbridge, then another stream and an old road. Pines end. Ahead, Trail undulates through hickory, maple, and chestnut oak.

2.4 Cross Spout Run, in deep, narrow ravine. Ahead, cross badly eroded, old road and ascend. (Old road, path, leads 0.2 mi to church located 0.1 mi from realigned Va 604.)

3.0 Peak of ridge.

3.1 Lookout Point, on left, has excellent winter view (partly obstructed in summer) of mountains to south. Possible campsite.

3.5 Cross old road.

3.6 Cross branch of Spout Run. Ahead 35 yd, blue-blazed trail on left leads 90 yd to intermittent *Sawmill Spring* and to Sam Moore Shelter. Turn right and ascend very steeply.

4.0 Top of Tomblin Hill. (Land records confirm the unusual spelling of this place name.) Ahead 40 yd pass extensive area of ant mounds on right. (*Don't stop here*, for ants cover the Trail as well!)

4.3 Cross old road in Fent Wiley Hollow, a broad, dark hollow with a great variety of mature trees.

4.5 Cross creek with two streams. Ahead, cross old road and pass old still site (in woods to left), and ascend.

4.5 Top of small ridge that divides the hollow. Descend and cross three streams ahead.

4.6 Turn right onto old road and ascend, very steeply at times.

5.0 Side trail on right leads 40 yd to rocky summit of Buzzard Hill. Nice view to west. Descend, very steeply in one place ahead.

5.3 Bear right onto old forest road.

5.6 Pass ruined foundation of an old cabin on right. Ahead 50 yd is a *spring* on left, beside Trail.

5.9 Bear right at minor *spring* on left and descend very steeply with rocky footing.

6.0 Cross main creek in Reservoir Hollow. (A falls is 160 yd upstream.)

6.5 Level, then descend ahead.

6.8 Leave woods and cross Va 605. (Mt. Weather, a FEMA facility, on Va 601, is about 1.4 mi to left.) After re-entering woods, descend steeply, then more gradually.

7.0 Pass through outcrops. Slight southward view from rocks.

7.3 Cross footbridge over Morgan Mill Stream in Ashby Hollow. Hemlocks. Ahead, cross dirt road still in use and ascend, very steeply at times, through chestnut oak and pine.

8.2 Knoll on Piney Ridge. Descend to saddle between two peaks.

8.3 Secondary peak on Piney Ridge. Descend, very steeply at times.

8.8 Cross creek in Bolden Hollow and bear left onto old forest road. Ahead in 125 yd turn right as series of switchbacks help ease 400-ft ascent to next peak.

9.3 Narrow ridge with limited view from rocky area 30 yd to right.

9.5 From local high point, descend, steeply at times, passing through rock outcrops ahead.

10.2 Blue-blazed Fishers Hill Loop Trail on right ascends Fishers Hill and after 0.8 mi rejoins *AT* at 10.9 mi.

10.5 Blue-blazed trail on right leads 0.1 mi to Rod Hollow Shelter and *spring*. Ahead 70 yd, cross stream and begin ascent. Pass old mine pits on both sides of Trail.

10.9 On ridge line, Fishers Hill Loop Trail rejoins *AT* from right.

11.3 Cross old stone wall then a stream in Duke Hollow and ascend through yellow poplar forest.

11.8 Pass unblazed path on right leading 0.2 mi to back side of Myron Glaser Cabin, reserved for PATC members only.

12.1 Cross creek.

12.3 Blue-blazed trail on right leads 0.2 mi to Myron Glaser Cabin.

12.7 Cross creek.

13.3 Cross underground telephone cable right-of-way; clear to left, overgrown to right.

13.9 Blue-blazed trail leads left 85 yd to PATC trailhead parking lot. In 25 yd cross stream.

14.1 Leave woods. Cross US 50 bearing slightly right. Section ends at post in median strip of US 50, 0.25 mi west of Ashby Gap. (Restaurant is 0.8 mi west.) To continue on Trail, cross US 50 bearing slightly right and take path into woods.

Detailed Trail Data—South to North

0.0 Section begins at median strip of US 50, 0.25 mi west of Ashby Gap. (Restaurant 0.8 mi to west.) Cross US 50 bearing slightly right. Enter woods and ascend through dense undergrowth, elms, and lots of dogwood.

0.2 Cross stream. Ahead 25 yd, blue-blazed trail leads right 85 yd to PATC trailhead parking lot.

0.8 Cross underground telephone cable right-of-way.

1.5 Cross creek.

1.8 Blue-blazed trail on left leads 0.2 mi to Myron Glaser Cabin, reserved for PATC members only.

2.0 Cross creek.

2.3 Pass unblazed path on left leading 0.2 mi to back side of Glaser Cabin.

2.8 Cross stream in Duke Hollow. Ahead, cross old stone wall and ascend steeply past beeches.

3.2 On ridge line, Fishers Hill Loop Trail, on left, ascends Fishers Hill and after 0.8 mi rejoins *AT* at 3.9 mi. *AT* descends, passing old mine pits on both sides of Trail.

3.6 Cross two streams in Rod Hollow and in 70 yd blue-blazed trail on left leads 0.1 mi to Rod Hollow Shelter and *spring*.

3.9 Fishers Hill Loop Trail rejoins *AT* from left.

4.6 Reach local high point.

4.8 Narrow ridge with limited view from rocky area 30 yd to left. *AT* follows series of switchbacks, some of which are old forest roads, in making 400-ft descent to Bolden Hollow.

5.3 Bear right off forest road and cross creek in Bolden Hollow. Ahead, ascend very steeply.

5.8 Reach secondary peak of Piney Ridge. Descend into saddle between 2 peaks.

5.9 Knoll on Piney Ridge. Descend, very steeply at times, through pine and chestnut oak.

6.8 Cross dirt road still in use in Ashby Hollow. Ahead, cross footbridge over Morgan Mill Stream and ascend. Hemlocks.

7.1 Pass through outcrops. Slight southward view from rocks. Ascend gradually ahead, then steeply.

7.3 Cross Va 605 and cross powerline right-of-way. (Mt. Weather, on Va 601, is about 1.4 mi to right.) Then enter woods and ascend.

7.6 After short level area, descend gradually, then steeply, through many beeches.

8.1 Cross main creek in Reservoir Hollow. A falls is 160 yd upstream. Ascend very steeply.

8.2 Bear left at small *spring* on right. Level ahead.

8.5 *Spring* on right, beside Trail. Ahead 50 yd pass ruined foundation of old cabin on left.

8.8 Bear left off old forest road and onto path. Ahead, ascend gradually, then very steeply.

9.1 Side trail on left leads 40 yd to rocky summit of Buzzard Hill. Nice view to west. Descend, very steeply at times.

9.5 Turn left off road and onto path. Ahead, cross three streams in Fent Wiley Hollow and ascend.

9.6 Top of small ridge that divides hollow. Descend into broad, dark hollow with a great variety of mature trees.

Ahead, pass old still site (in woods to right) and cross old road.

9.7 Cross creek with two streams. Then cross old forest road. Ascend steeply ahead.

10.1 Pass through extensive area of ant mounds on left. *Don't stop here,* for ants cover the Trail as well. Ahead 40 yd pass top of Tomblin Hill. (Land records confirm the unusual spelling of this place name.)

10.5 Blue-blazed trail straight ahead leads 90 yd to intermittent *Sawmill Spring* and to Sam Moore Shelter. Turn left and in 35 yd cross a branch of Spout Run. Ascend steeply.

10.6 Cross old road.

11.0 Lookout Point, on right, has excellent winter view (partly obstructed in summer) of mountains to south. Possible campsite.

11.1 Peak of ridge.

11.7 Cross badly eroded, old road, then cross Spout Run, in deep, narrow ravine. (Old road, path, leads left 0.2 mi to church located 0.1 mi from realigned Va 604.) Ahead, after a steep ascent, trail undulates through hickory, maple and chestnut oak.

12.9 Cross old forest road. Ahead, cross stream, and then cross creek on footbridge. Ascend ahead, steeply at times, through pines.

13.2 Blue-blazed trail on right leads 125 yd to *spring*.

13.4 Path on right leads 0.2 mi to Bears Den Hostel.

13.5 Bears Den Rocks on left has outstanding view of Shenandoah Valley. (Path on right leads 0.2 mi to Bears Den Hostel. *Tap water* available.) Ahead, descend generally through oak, laurel, sassafras, yellow poplar, and dogwood.

14.0 Turn left on shoulder of Va 7. (Bluemont is 1.8 mi east of gap.)

14.1 End of section at median strip of Va 679. To continue on Trail enter small parking area at junction of Va 7 and Va 679 and ascend into woods.

Former farm above Trumbo Hollow

SECTION 4
ASHBY GAP TO MANASSAS GAP
Distance: 12.3 Miles

Road Approaches and Parking

Ashby Gap: This is on US 50. The *AT* crosses US 50
0.25 mi west of the gap. There is a PATC 10-car parking lot
on the west side of Va 601, about 0.2 mile north of Va 7. A
blue-blazed access trail at the back of the lot descends to the
AT in 85 yd (at 13.9/0.2 mi). Paris is 1.0 mile east and
Washington, D.C., is 56 miles east.

To reach Trico Tower Trail: From Va 55, at Manassas
Gap, take Va 638 north for about five miles. There is room
to park on the shoulder near the tower's access road. From
the tower, a blue-blazed trail leads south 0.4 mile to the *AT*
(at 8.1/4.4 mi), providing access for shorter hikes in this
section.

To reach G. Richard Thompson State Wildlife Management Area Parking: From Va 55, at Manassas Gap, take Va
638 north to Parking Area #4, on right. Blue-blazed Ted
Lake Trail follows old road 0.8 mile from here to *AT* (at
10.1/2.4 mi). Farther north on Va 638, Parking Area #7 lies
on the right at junction with Blue Mountain Road. A gated
old road leads right (east) 0.2 mile from here to *AT* (at
6.8/5.7 mi). There is another parking area near the *AT* on
Signal Knob, but the road to it is not driveable for most cars.

To reach Sky Meadows State Park: See chapter on "Side
Trails."

Manassas Gap: This is on Va 55, at Linden. The *AT*
crosses Va 55 about a mile east of Linden, at the junction
with Va 725. From the east, on I-66, exit onto Va 55 at the
Linden exit. The *AT*, going north, follows Va 725. There is
room for several cars to park by the junction. Markham is
about 3.4 miles east, Front Royal is about 7.1 miles west,
and Washington, D.C., is 65 miles away.

Points of Interest

This section has an excellent view from a cleared slope (at 4.1/8.2 mi) and interesting rock outcrops (at 10.8/1.7 mi). The Trico Firetower vicinity (0.4 mi by side trail, at 8.1/4.4 mi) is noted for its profuse growth of trillium.

Maps

PATC Map 8 and USGS Paris, Upperville, and Linden Quadrangles

Shelters and Campgrounds

Sky Meadows State Park (1.3 mi by side trail, at 3.1/9.4 mi) has camping at designated sites and a shelter. Nightly fee per campsite (limited to six persons per site) is $8.00. See chapter on "Side Trails."

Dick's Dome Shelter (0.2 mi by side trail, at 5.4/7.1 mi), beside Whiskey Hollow Creek, accommodates four. Privy on hillside, a short distance above. Taking water from the creek is not advisable. PATC member Dick George built this shelter on private land for *AT* hikers.

Manassas Gap Shelter (70 yd by side trail, at 10.1/2.4 mi) accommodates six persons and has a *spring* nearby.

Public Accommodations

There is a restaurant 0.8 mi west of Ashby Gap.

Supplies

A post office, small store, and telephone are at the junction of Va 55 and Va 638, at Manassas Gap (Linden).

Water is available from *springs* at 4.4/8.1 mi and at Manassas Gap Shelter, and from Sky Meadows State Park.

Brief Description

As in Virginia Section 3, the *AT* in this section has been relocated onto publicly acquired land in recent years. As a consequence of these relocations, and because a road follows the ridge crest, the Trail now snakes along the slopes, dipping in and out of numerous ravines. Although the footing is generally good, these undulations make this a moderately difficult day hike.

Except for an outstanding view and odd rock formation, this section has no features of particular interest. There is, however, a great variety of flora: orchards, sapling forests, jungles of vines, and lots of wildflowers.

Much of the land in this section is part of the G. Richard Thompson Wildlife Management Area, which is under the jurisdiction of the Virginia Commission of Game and Inland Fisheries. Hunters may pose a danger during season.

Side Trails

To Sky Meadows State Park (at 3.1/9.4 mi)
To Dick's Dome Shelter (at 5.4/7.1 mi)
Trico Tower Trail (at 8.1/4.4 mi)
To Manassas Gap Shelter (at 10.1/2.4 mi)
Ted Lake Trail (at 10.1/2.4 mi)

Detailed Trail Data—North to South

0.0 Section begins at median strip of US 50, 0.25 mi west of Ashby Gap. (Restaurant 0.8 mi west.) Cross US 50 bearing slightly right. Enter woods on path. Cross stone wall and turn right onto old road with high grass. A sign says that George Washington once passed here.

0.2 Trail turns sharply left and ascends through profuse dogwood followed by a dense tangle of vines.

0.7 Pass rock piles on left, in former cleared field. Good campsite.

0.9 Cross telephone cable right-of-way.

1.2 At sharp bend in gravel road, turn left off road and ascend on old roadbed.

1.3 Turn right, off road and onto path, just before reaching gate. Descend ahead on a 50-foot-wide corridor of public land. *Stay on Trail.* The owner of the adjacent land often patrols the private, parallel road.

1.7 Turn right onto dirt road.

1.8 Turn left onto grassy road and ascend steeply. Interesting growth, with lots of locust trees.

2.4 Bear right and descend.

2.5 Turn left and ascend by a few long switchbacks.

2.7 Cross gravel road.

2.8 Turn right onto gravel road and immediately cross gas pipeline right-of-way. Good westward view. As road leaves clearing turn left into woods. Trail enters Sky Meadows State Park.

3.0 Generally level Trail bears away from pipeline corridor and passes through dense growth of young trees.

3.1 Blue-blazed trail on left leads 1.7 mi to Sky Meadows State Park Visitors Center, or 1.3 mi to park campground. See chapter on "Side Trails."

3.4 Enter the G. Richard Thompson State Wildlife Management Area. The *AT* passes through the Management Area for most of the next 7.3 miles. Hunters may pose a danger during season.

3.6 Hunters' path on right leads 0.1 mi downhill to parking lot for 10 cars.

4.1 Enter large overgrown clearing with growth of sumac. Excellent view to south and southeast. Trail blazed on tall poles.

4.2 Spur trail on right leads 0.1 mi to parking lot for 20 cars on Signal Knob. (Signal Knob was the site of a Civil War signal station. The Strother family cemetery is on the eastern slope of the ridge.) Continue straight.

4.3 Enter woods.

4.4 Pass *spring* on left. Road has a pleasant canopy of shrubs.

4.9 Turn right, off road and onto path, leaving Game Commission land and entering land purchased for the Trail by the State of Virginia. Descend steeply.

5.3 Cross wide dirt road.

5.4 Cross creek in Whiskey Hollow. In 70 yd, blue-blazed trail on left leads 0.2 mi to Dick's Dome Shelter. Ascend steeply by switchbacks, re-entering Game Commission land.

6.0 Pass lone boulder and ascend more moderately.

6.5 Reach level crest.

6.6 Go left at fork off road and descend.

6.8 Turn left onto old road. Just ahead, cross old road in clearing. (To right, road leads 0.2 mi to Parking Area #7.)

7.1 Bear right where abandoned trail intersects on left. Ahead, ascend very steeply, then more gradually.

7.6 Turn left onto dirt road, then almost immediately turn right off road and ascend very steeply. (To right, road leads 0.7 mi to Va 638, just south of Trico Firetower.)

7.9 Blue-blazed Trico Tower Trail leads right 0.5 mi to Trico (Tri-County) Firetower. (Built by the CCC in 1934, the 70-foot tower stands, at 2,207 feet, on the highest point in this section. *The tower should not be climbed.* The surrounding trees have now grown so high that no view is available except from the highest levels, and the decaying condition of the wooden stairs renders them extremely dangerous.)

8.6 Cross intermittent stream and ascend ahead.

9.0 Turn left onto dirt road. (Road leads right 0.4 mi to Va 638.) In 90 yd, turn right off road.

9.8 Pass chimney ruins on left. Blue-blazed trail leads left 70 yd to Manassas Gap Shelter and *spring*. Ahead, turn left at crossroads. (To right, the Game Commission's blue-blazed Ted Lake Trail leads 0.8 mi to Parking Area #4.) Go 90 yd and turn right into woods. Ascend through hickory, sassafras, oak, yellow poplar.

10.0 Turn right, off road and onto path, at edge of small game clearing. Trail undulates ahead around right side of knob.

10.3 Leave G. Richard Thompson Wildlife Management Area. Descend, passing dense undergrowth and dogwood.

10.4 Trail passes between interesting rock formations. Monolithic outcrops jut up from the ground.

10.6 Old stone wall on left. Continue to descend through rocky areas.

11.3 Blue-blazed trail leads left to view from hillside.

11.4 Begin descent with switchbacks.

11.7 After stone steps, cross meadow and dam below pond. Turn right then left across farm land and up wooden steps.

11.9 Top of small ridge. Descend with switchbacks.

12.1 Cross massive footbridge built to withstand heavy spring runoff, pass through PATC trailhead parking lot, and turn left on Va 725.

12.3 Intersect Va 55 after passing under I-66 overpasses. (Linden, in Manassas Gap, is about 1.0 mi to right on level route. It has a post office, small store, and telephone at junction with Va 638. Also at junction is Discovery Monument, commemorating the supposed site from which John Lederer first saw the Shenandoah Valley in 1670.) To continue on Trail, cross Va 55 and enter woods to right of junction.

Detailed Trail Data—South to North

0.0 Junction of Va 55 and Va 725. Follow Va 725, passing under I-66 overpasses. (Linden, in Manassas Gap, is about 1.0 mi to left on level route. It has a post office, small store, and telephone at junction with Va 638. Also at junction is Discovery Monument, commemorating the supposed site from which John Lederer first saw the Shenandoah Valley in 1670.)

0.2 Turn right off Va 725 and cross PATC trailhead parking lot. Cross massive footbridge built to withstand heavy spring runoff.

0.4 Top of small ridge. Descend.

0.5 Wooden steps. Cross old farm lane, turn right then left. Cross dam below pond, then meadow.

0.9 Stone steps; begin ascent with switchbacks.

1.0 Blue-blazed trail leads right to view from hillside.

1.3 Old road intersects on right. Go straight. Old stone wall on right. Just ahead, turn right, off road and onto path.

1.7 Old stone wall on right; ascend through rocky areas.

1.9 Trail passes between interesting rock formations. Monolithic outcrops jut up from ground.

2.0 Enter the G. Richard Thompson Wildlife Management Area. The *AT* passes through the Management Area for most of the next 7.3 mi. Hunters may pose a danger during season. Trail undulates ahead around left side of knob.

2.3 Turn left onto old road at edge of small game clearing. Descend ahead through hickory, sassafras, oak, and yellow poplar.

2.5 Turn left on blue-blazed Ted Lake Trail and in 90 yd turn right at cross roads. (Ted Lake Trail continues straight ahead 0.8 mi to Parking Area #4.) Ahead, blue-blazed trail leads right 70 yd to Manassas Gap Shelter and *spring*. Then pass chimney ruins on right and ascend steeply.

2.9 Level, then descend ahead.

3.3 Turn left onto dirt road. In 90 yd, turn right off road and onto path. (Road continues 0.4 mi to Va 638.)

3.7 Cross intermittent stream. Trail ascends, then becomes level ahead.

4.4 Blue-blazed Trico Tower Trail leads left 0.4 mi to Trico (Tri-County) Firetower. (Built by the CCC in 1934, the 70-foot tower stands, at 2,207 feet, on the highest point in this section. *The tower should not be climbed.* The surrounding trees have now grown so high that no view is available except from the highest levels, and the decaying condition of the wooden stairs renders them extremely dangerous.) Descend very steeply.

4.7 Turn left onto dirt road, then almost immediately turn right off road and descend. (To left, road leads 0.7 mi to Va 638, just south of Trico Firetower.)

5.2 Bear left where abandoned trail intersects on right. Ascend.

5.5 Cross old road in clearing. (To left, road leads 0.2 mi to Parking Area #7.) Then turn right off road and onto path.

5.7 Bear right onto old road. Level, then descend.

6.3 Pass lone boulder on right and descend very steeply.

6.9 Blue-blazed trail on right leads 0.2 mi to Dick's Dome Shelter. Then cross creek in Whiskey Hollow, leaving Game Commission land and entering land purchased for the Trail by the State of Virginia. Ascend.

7.0 Cross wide dirt road.

7.4 Turn left onto old road, re-entering Game Commission land. Road has a pleasant canopy of shrubs ahead.

7.9 Pass *spring* on right and enter large clearing with heavy growth of sumac.

8.0 Path leads left 0.1 mi to 20-car parking area on Signal Knob, maintained by the Game Commission. (Signal Knob was site of a Civil War signal station. Strother family cemetery is on eastern slope of knob.) Bear right, with excellent view to south and southeast.

8.2 Enter woods and descend on path, then ascend.

8.9 Leave Game Commission land and enter Sky Meadows State Park. Pass path which leads 0.1 mi to 10-car parking lot.

9.2 Blue-blazed trail on right leads 1.7 mi to Sky Meadows State Park Visitor Center, or 1.3 mi to park campground. See chapter on "Side Trails." Ahead, Trail passes through dense growth of young trees.

9.3 Trail bears left and parallels gas pipeline right-of-way.

9.4 Turn right onto former fire road, leaving Sky Meadows State Park, and cross pipeline corridor. Good westward view. In 50 yd, turn left, off road and onto path, and descend. Do not attempt to shortcut on the fire road, which is private property posted "No Trespassing." The landowner often patrols the road.

9.6 Cross gravel road.

9.8 Turn right onto road.

9.9 Bear left off road and onto path.

10.5 Turn right onto dirt road.

10.6 Turn left off road and onto path. This is a 50-foot-wide corridor of public land. *Stay on Trail.*

11.0 Turn left onto dirt road and descend steeply.

11.1 Turn right at crossroads and descend more gradually. In 70 yd, turn left off road and onto path.

11.4 Cross telephone cable right-of-way.

11.6 Pass rock piles on right, in former cleared field. Descend ahead through a dense tangle of vines, then through profuse dogwood.

12.1 Trail turns sharply right and ascends on old road with high grass. Ahead, a sign says that George Washington once passed here.

12.3 Turn left off road and cross stone wall to US 50 and end of section at median of US 50 in Ashby Gap. (Restaurant 0.8 mi west.) To continue on Trail, bear to right 0.25 mi, and enter woods.

SECTION 5
MANASSAS GAP TO CHESTER GAP
Distance: 8.2 Miles

Road Approaches and Parking

Manassas Gap: This is on Va 55, at Linden. The *AT* crosses Va 55 about 1.0 mile east of Linden, at the junction with Va 725. From the east, on I-66, exit onto Va 55 at Markham. From the west, on I-66, get onto Va 55 at the Linden exit. The *AT*, going south, enters the woods just a few yards west of the junction. There is room for several cars to park by the junction. Markham is about 3.4 miles east, Front Royal is about 7.1 miles west, and Washington, D.C., is about 65 miles away.

Va 638: There is no parking near this crossing.

US 522: The *AT* crosses this highway at a point 1.5 miles west of Chester Gap and 3.2 miles east of Va 55, in Front Royal. Washington, D.C., via I-66 and Front Royal, is about 74 miles away. There is room for several cars to park on the south side of the highway at the *AT* crossing.

Points of Interest

The highlight of this section is an abandoned farm on top of a mountain with outstanding views in several directions (at 1.2/7.0 mi).

Maps

PATC Map 8 and USGS Linden and Front Royal Quadrangles

Shelter and Campgrounds

The Jim and Molly Denton Shelter (50 yd by side trail, at 3.0/5.2 mi) accommodates 7 persons under the roof and has a large porch with a wooden bench. Other facilities include privy, *spring*, shower, covered picnic table, fireplace, protected wood supply, and tent platforms.

Mosby Campsite (100 yd by side trail, at 4.9/3.3 mi) has several places for tents and a nearby *spring*, but no other facilities.

Supplies

A post office, telephone, and small store are at the junction of Va 55 and Va 638, at Manassas Gap (Linden).

Water is available from a *spring*, at 3.0/5.2 mi, and from *Tom Sealock Spring* (125 yd by side trail, at 4.9/3.3 mi).

Brief Description

From either direction, this section poses a nearly 1,000-foot ascent along the slopes of High Knob and a 600-foot ascent of a neighboring mountain. The ascents are somewhat steeper from the south. The footing is generally good. This section can be combined with Virginia Section 6 for a moderate day hike, if hiked from south to north.

Side Trails

To Denton Shelter and campground (at 3.0/5.2 mi)

To Mosby Campsite and *Tom Sealock Spring* (at 4.9/3.3 mi)

Detailed Trail Data—North to South

0.0 Junction of Va 55 and Va 725. Enter woods through weedy area to right of junction. Ahead, a boardwalk crosses several channels of Goose Creek, with beaver dams and activity on right. Beyond the boardwalk, a bulletin board posted on tree at left has Trail information. (Linden, in Manassas Gap, is about 1.0 mi to right on level route. It has a post office, small store, and telephone at junction with Va 638. Also at junction is Discovery Monument, commemorating the supposed site from which John Lederer first saw the Shenandoah Valley in 1670.)

0.1 Cross railroad tracks and ascend steeply.

0.5 Cross faint old road, then turn right onto old road at junction. Go left at fork in a few yards.

0.7 Switchback steeply to left at base of large cliff.

0.8 Switchback to right over boulders.

0.9 Enter old orchard, part of abandoned farm on top of mountain. Go straight, with good view of High Knob.

1.0 Turn right onto old, sunken road and follow white-blazed posts.

1.1 Pass building and ascend cleared hill.

1.2 Excellent view down Trumbo Hollow from top of hill. Cross center of field, bearing slightly right from the center to the next post. Superb winter view, through gap, of Shenandoah Valley and West Virginia mountains beyond.

1.3 Leave clearing and descend. Ahead, cross stile and ascend. Cross over crest of ridge, not along it, through an old field that is becoming overgrown. Descend ahead, with view of High Knob.

1.6 Turn right and descend on old road.

1.7 Bear left off road at edge of former farm. Go around left side of corral. Descend very steeply through pasture toward graveled farm road.

1.9 Cross stile at left of gate and turn left onto paved Va 638. *Watch for traffic.* In 70 yd, turn right off road a few yards after driveway on left. Ahead, small bulletin board, posted on tree on right, has Trail information. Pass through overgrown field.

2.1 Cross bridge over small stream. Ascend, generally steeply. Ahead, Trail levels off as dense undergrowth replaces mature trees.

2.4 Go straight where another path forks to left in small clearing.

2.5 Turn right, leaving path that follows ridge crest. Trail undulates ahead, and mature trees return.

2.6 Cross old stone wall. Ascend ahead.

2.9 Old road intersects on right. Go straight.

3.0 Trail on right leads 50 yd to Denton Shelter and campground. Ahead, go straight at crossroads. *Do not enter* ruined old house on right. A *spring* lies a few yards to left of house.

3.1 Turn right, off road and onto path, and descend briefly. Lots of hickory, including shagbark, and yellow poplar throughout area.

3.7 Base of small cliff.

4.2 Cross powerline right-of-way. Fair view to right. Ahead, pass through a very young forest dominated by dogwood. The lack of old trees suggests a former clearcut.

4.5 Cross dirt road.

4.6 Cross old road. Ahead, cross old stone wall.

4.7 Cross old road.

4.9 Blue-blazed trail leads left 100 yd to Mosby Campsite (primitive) and another 25 yd downhill to *Tom Sealock Spring*, named for one of Col. Mosby's men, who lived here after the Civil War. (The site is on ten acres of land donated to the PATC in 1965 by Mrs. Mary H. Keyser. PATC donated the land to the National Park Service in 1987. A former shelter on this site was apparently stolen in 1980 for the sake of its chestnut logs.) Ahead, cross stream and ascend. Spotted touch-me-nots may be seen here.

5.0 Cross Fire Road 3460.

5.1 Turn right onto old road.

5.4 Turn left off road and descend very steeply with rocky footing.

5.9 Enter Shenandoah National Park. To end of section, National Park Service easement passes over land belonging to the Research and Conservation Center. (The Center is a 4,000-acre wildlife preserve belonging to the National Zoological Park, an agency of the Smithsonian Institution. The land was formerly a USDA livestock research station and, before that, a U.S. Cavalry remount post.) *Camping and hunting are prohibited.*

6.2 Go right at fork. Blue-blazed path on left is used for access by trail maintenance workers. Ahead, ticks are common.

6.3 Cross maintenance road.(Gate to zoo is on right.)

6.4 Turn right onto old road.

6.5 Turn left off road and onto path. Pass through area of dense undergrowth ahead.

6.8 Descend gradually.

7.4 Cross Bear Hollow Creek.

7.9 Just after gravel road intersects on right, turn right between the two fences. Trail undulates through scrub between fences, paralleling highway. View of Lake Front Royal across highway.

8.2 Turn left, almost immediately turn right, and reach US 522. To continue on Trail, cross US 522.

Detailed Trail Data—South to North

0.0 US 522. Ascend embankment and parallel highway. In 30 yd, turn left and almost immediately turn right. Pass through scrub ahead, with view of Lake Front Royal across highway. (For the first 2.3 mi, Trail follows a National Park Service easement over land belonging to the Research and Conservation Center. The Center is a 4,000-acre wildlife preserve belonging to the National Zoological Park, an agency of Smithsonian Institution. The land was formerly a USDA livestock research station and, before that, a U.S. Cavalry remount post.) *Camping and hunting are prohibited.* Ticks are common in this area.

0.3 Turn left onto gravel road, then bear right onto grassy old road, between fence and Bear Hollow Creek.

0.8 Cross creek.

1.4 Ascend steeply through area of dense undergrowth.

1.7 Turn right onto old road.

1.8 Turn left off road and onto path. Ahead, cross old road.

2.0 Bear left. Blue-blazed trail on right is used for access by trail maintenance workers.

2.3 Trail leaves National Zoological Park land, but continues on National Park Service land.

2.5 Descend steeply.

2.7 Ascend very steeply with rocky footing.

2.8 Turn right onto road and descend.

3.1 Turn left off road and onto path.

3.2 Cross Fire Road 3460.

3.3 Cross stream. Spotted touch-me-knots may be seen here. In 70 yd, go left at fork. (Blue-blazed trail leads right 100 yd to Mosby Campsite, primitive, and another 25 yd downhill to *Tom Sealock Spring*, named for one of Col. Mosby's men, who lived here after the Civil War. The site is on ten acres of land donated to the PATC in 1965 by Mrs. Mary H. Keyser. PATC donated the land to the National Park Service in 1987. A former shelter on this site was apparently stolen in 1980 for the sake of its chestnut logs.)

3.5 Cross old road. Ahead, cross old stone wall.

3.6 Cross old road.

3.7 Cross old road. Ahead, pass through a very young forest dominated by dogwood. The lack of old trees suggests a former clearcut.

4.1 Cross powerline right-of-way. Fair view to left.

4.5 Small cliff on left. Descend ahead through lots of hickory, including shagbark, and yellow poplar.

5.1 Turn left onto road.

5.2 Go straight at crossroads. *Do not enter* old house on left. A *spring* lies a few yards to left of house. Ahead, trail on left leads 50 yd to Denton Shelter and campground.

5.3 Go right at fork.

5.6 Cross old stone wall. Trail undulates ahead.

5.7 Turn left at junction. Dense undergrowth replaces mature trees. Descend ahead.

5.8 Trail intersects on right in small clearing. Go straight.

6.1 Cross bridge over small stream. Pass through overgrown field ahead.

6.3 Turn left onto paved Va 638. *Watch for traffic.* A small bulletin board, posted on tree on left just before turn, has Trail information. In 70 yd, turn right off road and onto graveled farm road. Then, cross stile at right of gate. Follow line of trees steeply up hill to right side of corral.

6.5 Turn right onto old road and ascend.

6.6 Turn left off road. Ahead, view of High Knob to rear.

6.8 Cross over crest of ridge, through an old field that is becoming overgrown. Descend and cross stile ahead.

6.9 Enter cleared field of former farm on mountain top. Cross center of field and descend. Superb winter view on left, through gap, of Shenandoah Valley and the West Virginia mountains beyond. Ahead, excellent view down Trumbo Hollow. Follow white-blazed posts.

7.1 Pass building. Ascend sunken farm road ahead.

7.2 Turn left off road and cross old orchard.

7.3 Leave orchard, enter woods, and descend ahead over boulders.

7.4 Switchback to left and descend steeply.

7.5 Switchback to right at base of large cliff.

7.7 Go straight onto old road, which intersects from left, and then turn left, off road and onto path, in a few yards. Ahead, cross faint old road.

8.1 Cross railroad tracks. A small bulletin board posted on tree to right has Trail information; beyond, a boardwalk crosses several channels of Goose Creek, with beaver dams and activity on left.

8.2 Junction of Va 55 and Va 725. (Linden, in Manassas Gap, is about 1.0 mi to left on level route. It has a post office, small store, and telephone at junction with Va 638.

Also at junction is Discovery Monument, commemorating the supposed site from which John Lederer first saw the Shenandoah Valley in 1670.) To continue on Trail, cross Va 55 and follow Va 725.

Hikers Beware!

SECTION 6
CHESTER GAP TO
SHENANDOAH NATIONAL PARK

Distance: 3.6 Miles

Road Approaches and Parking

US 522: The *AT* crosses this highway at a point 1.5 miles west of Chester Gap and 3.2 miles east of Va 55, in Front Royal. Washington, D.C., via I-66 and Front Royal, is about 74 miles away. There is room for several cars to park on the south side of the highway.

To reach Va 602 and Va 601: From US 522, between Front Royal and the *AT* crossing, take paved Va 604 south. Graveled Va 602 forks to the left; room for two cars to park. Farther ahead on Va 604, graveled Va 601 forks to the left. Va 601 has a parking area (on PATC land) on the right, marked by a sign, with room for about four cars. A blue-blazed access trail, opposite, ascends 0.2 mi to the *AT*.

To reach Shenandoah National Park boundary: From US 522, turn onto crescent road on south side of Chester Gap. Turn onto Va 610 and follow it to gate at Park boundary. There is room for several cars to park here. Continue on foot up dirt road (old Compton Gap Road) for 0.5 mi. Then turn right onto *AT* and descend another 0.2 mi to Park boundary, at southern end of Section 6.

Points of Interest

There are two good views (at 1.7/1.9 mi, and 3.6/0.0 mi). The variety of growth is also interesting.

Maps

PATC Map 9 and USGS Front Royal and Chester Gap Quadrangles

Shelters and Campgrounds
Tom Floyd Wayside (short distance by side trail, at 2.9/0.7 mi) has shelter and lies 0.2 mi uphill from *Ginger Spring*. Use is free on a first-come, first-served basis. *Camp fires and group camping are prohibited.* Users must carry out all trash.

Supplies
Water is available from outside tap at closed Northern Virginia Trail Center (0.1 mi by side trail at 1.2/2.4) and at *Ginger Spring* (0.2 mi by side trail, at 2.6/1.0 mi).

Brief Description
From north to south, this section has 1,600 feet of ascent and only 300 feet of descent. The footing is very good. This section can be combined with Virginia Section 5 for a moderate day hike, if hiked from south to north.

Side Trails
Access trail from Va 601 (at 2.6/1.0 mi)
To *Ginger Spring* (at 2.6/1.0 mi)
To Tom Floyd Wayside (at 2.6/0.7 mi)

Detailed Trail Data—North to South
0.0 US 522. Descend and cross footbridge over polluted Sloan Creek. The Trail ahead follows a National Park Service easement over land belonging to Research and Conservation Center. (The Center is a 4,000-acre wildlife preserve belonging to the National Zoological Park, an agency of the Smithsonian Institution. The land was formerly a USDA livestock research station and, before that, a U.S. Cavalry remount post.) *Camping and hunting are prohibited.*
0.1 Cross footbridge over polluted marsh. Ascend, steeply at times, with fenced meadow and good view on right. (A World War II prisoner-of-war camp was on top of the ridge

above the former cavalry post.) Ticks are common in this area. Frequent inspections for ticks are recommended.

0.5 Enter woods dominated by yellow poplars (tuliptrees).

0.7 Just before crossing ditch, evening orchids may be seen beside large yellow poplar.

0.9 Cross crest of spur ridge. Descend steeply.

1.2 Blue-blazed trail leads left 0.1 mi to tap *water* and tent sites at former Northern Virginia Trail Center (now closed).

1.4 Cross Va 602. (Enter land owned by Virginia Polytechnic Institute. Northern Virginia 4-H Center is 0.3 mi to right and turn up driveway. *Water* available all year; showers and pool open Mem. Day to Labor Day. Showers free, pool fee $2.) Trail undulates ahead through forest where beech trees predominate. In 50 yd, cross Moore Run. *Do not take water from here or at the stream ahead*, for there are houses upstream.

1.5 Cross intermittent stream and ascend.

1.7 Good view of Harmony Hollow from bench.

1.8 Enter woods again.

1.9 Giant beech on right. Oak, hickory, sassafras forest.

2.0 Bear left. (Old *A.T.*, now closed, bears right.

2.6 Bear left. (Blue-blazed trail to right leads 0.3 mi to Va 601. PATC parking lot is 0.3 mi downhill, north, on Va 601.) Just ahead is first of three spur trails leading right into Tom Floyd Wayside and *Ginger Spring*. Tent sites here.

2.9 Third spur trail leads right to Tom Floyd Wayside Shelter and tent sites.

3.3 Ridge crest. Level, descend ahead.

3.4 Cross old road and ascend.

3.5 Ascend steeply up cliff.

3.6 Possums Rest. 180-degree view west from top of cliff. Turn left and reach boundary of Shenandoah National Park in 50 yd. Compton Road junction lies 0.2 mi ahead.

Detailed Trail Data—South to North

0.0 Shenandoah National Park boundary. Reach Possums Rest in 50 yd. 180-degree view west from top of cliff. Turn right and descend cliff steeply. (Trail ahead is on the Harmony Hollow scenic easement, first such easement established in Virginia.)

0.1 Bottom of cliff. Descend ahead through oak and hickory forest.

0.2 Cross old road and ascend.

0.7 Path on left leads to Tom Floyd Wayside Shelter and tent sites. (Backcountry permits available here, self-serve.) Pass through extensive growth of white ash and yellow poplar (tuliptree). Ahead, two more spur trails lead left to campsites.

1.0 Third spur trail, blue-blazed, leads to tent sites and in 0.2 mi to *Ginger Spring*. Ahead, a strong aroma of sassafras may be detectable in places. Then bear right. (Blue-blazed trail straight ahead leads 0.3 mi to Va 601.)

1.6 Continue straight as old *A.T.* now closed, goes left.

1.7 Giant beech on left.

1.9 Good view of Harmony Hollow from bench.

2.1 Cross intermittent stream. *Do not take water from here or at stream ahead*, for there are houses upstream. Trail undulates ahead through forest where beech trees predominate.

2.2 Cross Moore Run. In 50 yd, cross Va 602. (Northern Virginia 4-H Center is 0.3 mi to left to driveway uphill. *Water* available all year; showers and pool open Mem. Day to Labor Day. Showers free, pool fee $2.) Leave VPI land and enter land belonging to the Research and Conservation Center. (The Center is a 4,000-acre wildlife preserve belonging to the National Zoological Park, an agency of the Smithsonian Institution. The land was formerly a USDA livestock research station and, before that, a U.S. Cavalry remount post.) *Camping and hunting are prohibited*. Ascend steeply ahead.

2.4 Blue-blazed trail leads right 0.1 mi to tent sites and tap *water* at former Northern Virginia Trail Center, now closed.

2.7 Cross crest of spur ridge. Descend through forest dominated by yellow poplar.

2.9 Just after crossing ditch, evening orchids may be seen beside large yellow poplar.

3.1 Leave woods and descend, sometimes steeply, with fenced meadow and good view on left. (A World War II prisoner-of-war camp was on top of the ridge above the former cavalry post.) Ticks are common in this area. Frequent inspections for ticks are recommended.

3.5 Cross footbridge over polluted marsh, then cross footbridge over polluted Sloan Creek.

3.6 US 522 and end of section. To continue on Trail, cross US 522 and ascend embankment.

CHAPTER 8
SIDE TRAILS

The PATC maintains a number of blue-blazed side trails that either intersect or parallel the *AT*. They are noted in the "Detailed Trail Data" for each section. Most of these are short paths leading to shelters, or viewpoints, and do not require further description. The following trails, however, deserve a detailed description because of their particular features and/or the access to the *AT* that they provide.

The approximately 220-mile Tuscarora-Big Blue Trail provides a loop to the west of the *AT*. It intersects the *AT* at Blue Mountain, Pennsylvania, and in the northern section of Shenandoah National Park. Separate guidebooks to this trail have been published by the PATC and the Keystone Trails Association.

There are also numerous side trails in the Catoctin Mountains and in the Washington, D.C., suburbs, but these too are covered in separate guidebooks published by the PATC.

MARYLAND

BEAR SPRING CABIN TRAIL
Distance: 1.0 Mile

Cross-reference: Maryland Section 5
Access: From US Alt-40, take Marker Rd (or take Bolivar Rd, or Reno Monument Rd, to Marker Rd) and turn onto Mountain Church Rd. Turn right onto road beside Locust Valley First Church of God. Park in church parking lot. Parking is for cabin use only, not for day hiking.

From US 340, take Md 17 north. Turn left onto Gapland Rd in Burkittsville. Then turn right onto Mountain Church Rd and see above.

Detailed Trail Data—From Road

0.0 Junction beside church. Ascend road past house.

0.2 Pass pond on left, as road curves sharply to right.

0.3 Turn left off road and cross creek, reaching Bear Spring Cabin. Trail continues up hollow.

0.5 *Bear Spring.* Ascend more steeply ahead.

0.8 White Rocks Trail (see below) intersects on right. Continue ahead on old road with good winter view.

1.0 Junction with *AT*.

Detailed Trail Data—From AT

0.0 Junction with *AT*. Descend steeply; good winter view.

0.2 White Rocks Trail (see below) intersects on left.

0.5 *Bear Spring.* Descend more gradually.

0.7 Bear Spring Cabin. Bear to right of cabin, cross creek, and turn right onto dirt road.

0.8 As road curves sharply to left, pass pond on right.

1.0 Junction with Mountain Church Rd, beside Locust Valley First Church of God.

WHITE ROCKS TRAIL
Distance: 0.2 Mile

Cross-reference: Maryland Section 5 and Bear Spring Cabin Trail

Detailed Trail Data

0.0 Junction with Bear Spring Cabin Trail. Ascend gradually to foot of quartzite cliff, then scramble very steeply up rocks. *Slippery at all times.*

0.2 Junction with *AT*. View from very small outcrop is fair in summer, but excellent in winter. The prominent ridge in view is South Mountain. This directional illusion is the result of Lambs Knoll being offset to the east from the line of the ridge.

GRANT CONWAY TRAIL
(Maryland Heights Trail)

Distance: 4.6 Miles

This circuit trail is located in the Maryland section of Harpers Ferry National Historical Park, at the southern end of Elk Ridge, across the Potomac from Harpers Ferry. Dedicated to Grant Conway, a former PATC leader, the trail is outstanding for its natural beauty and historic features.

Although relatively short, the trail contains substantial climbs and descents. *Profuse poison ivy*, often overhanging the trail, may make hiking problematic from May through October.

Park regulations prohibit camping and fires. Rock climbers, but not hikers, are required to register with park rangers in Harpers Ferry.

Cross-reference: Maryland Section 7

Access: Three free parking areas exist on Sandy Hook Rd near the trailhead. From the parking at Harpers Ferry, cross Goodloe Byron Memorial Footbridge and turn left onto canal towpath. Cross footbridge over canal and cross Sandy Hook Rd. *Watch out for traffic.* Trail starts here at old road, marked by Grant Conway Trail sign. Distance from *AT* is 0.4 mi.

History Along the Trail

Elk Ridge was settled during the Revolutionary War by Scottish Highland deserters from the British Army, who later sent for their wives. They were shepherds, gardeners, and weavers by trade, and they earned a living here by truck gardening and charcoal burning for the local iron furnaces. Gradually most of them migrated to the valleys to be closer to other employment. The last settlers were evacuated during the Civil War.

Most of Elk Ridge was included in Samples Manor, a timber holding for charcoal. A narrow-gauge railroad ran along the ridge from near the Stone Fort to Solomons Gap. The horsedrawn coal carts were reversed on a turntable in Solomons Gap, where the charcoal was shipped by wagons to Antietam. Coking coal shipped by the Chesapeake & Ohio Canal replaced charcoal at the Antietam Ironworks in the late 1840s, and the rail line was abandoned.

The Grant Conway Trail passes over a portion of Elk Ridge known as Maryland Heights, which played an important role in the Civil War. When Lee invaded Maryland in 1862, he detailed Jackson to capture Harpers Ferry. Maryland Heights was abandoned after a short fight by Federal Col. Thomas H. Ford, who was later court-martialed. From these heights, Confederate Major General R. H. Anderson bombarded Harpers Ferry. The garrison surrendered after a short siege, September 13-15.

There are numerous points of historical interest along the trail, mostly on the eastern side of the loop. "Six-Gun Battery" was composed of six 30-pound Parrott siege guns and two 24-pound howitzers. Nearby is the site of the house where Col. Ford made his decision to evacuate Federal troops from the ridge. Farther ahead is "100-Pound Gun." This gun was mounted on a circular track, and Federal gunners once fired it at a stone school house four miles away, demolishing the structure and killing several Confederates within.

The Stone Fort on top of the ridge is constructed of large, shaped blocks of unmortared stone. It was built after 1862 as the anchor to the new Harpers Ferry defense system, and was to be the final refuge for the garrison in the event of another attack. There are parallel walls across the ridge, siege gun positions, three magazines, and low, outer stone walls to protect the infantry. To the northwest, Bakerton and Martinsburg, W.Va., may be seen on clear days. To the east are Pleasant Valley and South Mountain.

The signal station for communication with Washington, via Sugar Loaf Mountain and the widow's walk on the Emory house in Brightwood, is believed to have been located on a high point to the right of the trail. Albert D. Richardson (*Tales of the Secret Service,* 1865) tells of climbing to the signal station and fortifications with a pack train to supply water to troops.

Detailed Trail Data—Naval Battery Branch

0.0 Sandy Hook Rd. Ascend steeply on gated, dirt road, marked by "Grant Conway Trail" sign. Just ahead, turn right off road and onto path. Trail is blazed orange.

0.1 Pass rock outcrop on right, which appears to have been chiseled out, perhaps as a probe for ore. Just ahead, house ruins on left.

0.2 Turn right off road and onto path.

0.4 Naval Battery, built in May 1862, on right. Large earthworks for gun emplacements can be seen. Ahead, turn left and pass pit on right, a "Powder Magazine" according to sign.

0.5 Turn right onto road and reach junction with loop trail.

Detailed Trail Data—Loop, Clockwise

0.5 Junction with Naval Battery Branch. Turn left and ascend very steeply on old "Military Road."

1.3 Turn right off road and onto path. Ahead, pass earthworks and ammunition pits on both sides of trail.

1.7 Bear right where Elk Ridge Trail, (open 2.5 mi to Buggy Rocks only) intersects on left. Ahead, cross wall of Stone Fort and pass survey marker for summit of Maryland Heights, 1,475 feet.

2.3 Pass historical marker for "100-Pound Gun." Descend ahead.

2.4 Excellent winter view from rocks on left.

2.6 Pass ammunition pits and infantry defenses on left.

2.7 Unmarked path leads right into "Six-Gun Battery." Turn left.

2.9 Turn right at junction to complete loop. (Trail on left leads 0.5 mi to Overlook Cliff, with an outstanding view of Harpers Ferry and the rivers.)

3.1 End of loop, at junction with Naval Battery Branch. Total distance, including roundtrip to cliff and return to Sandy Hook Rd, is 4.6 mi.

Detailed Trail Data—Loop, Counterclockwise

0.5 Junction with Naval Battery Branch. Go straight and ascend very steeply.

0.7 Turn left onto intersecting trail to continue on loop. (Straight ahead, trail leads 0.5 mi to Overlook Cliff, with an outstanding view of Harpers Ferry and the rivers.)

0.9 Unmarked path leads straight ahead into "Six-Gun Battery." Turn right.

1.1 Pass ammunition pits and infantry defenses on right.

1.3 Excellent winter view from rocks on right.

1.4 Pass historical marker for "100-Pound Gun."

1.9 Pass survey marker for summit of Maryland Heights, 1,475 feet.

2.0 Cross wall of Stone Fort. Ahead, bear left where Elk Ridge Trail (open for 2.5 mi only to Buggy Rocks) intersects on right. Ahead, pass earthworks and ammunition pits on both sides of trail.

2.4 Turn left onto old "Military Road" and descend very steeply.

3.1 End of loop, at junction with Naval Battery Branch. Total distance, including roundtrip to cliff and return to Sandy Hook Rd, is 4.6 mi.

ELK RIDGE TRAIL
Distance: 2.5 Miles

This blue-blazed trail is a ridge walk to a rocky outcrop known as Buggy Rocks. This is a good picnic spot with a view of Pleasant Valley. The trail continues farther down the ridge but there is no access at the other end.

Cross-reference: Grant Conway Trail

Maps: PATC Map #6 and USGS Harpers Ferry and Keedysville Quadrangles

Access: From Grant Conway Trail.

Detailed Trail Data

0.0 Junction with Grant Conway Trail, on northern side of Stone Fort. Trail follows ridge with little change in elevation for nearly 2 miles.

2.0 Descend, steeply at times, on old road.

2.5 Go right at fork, off road and onto path, and soon reach Buggy Rocks, on right. Good view of Pleasant Valley. Return by same route. (Trail continues along ridge but their are no other viewpoints and there is no access to a road.)

VIRGINIA & WEST VIRGINIA

LOUDOUN HEIGHTS TRAIL
Distance: 3.2 Miles

This blue-blazed trail follows the former *AT* route past several excellent views and through an historic site in Harpers Ferry National Historical Park. *Park regulations prohibit camping and fires*. In conjunction with the *AT*, it provides a 6.9 mile circuit hike.

Cross-reference: Maryland Section 7 and Virginia Section 1

Detailed Trail Date—North to South

0.0 From the *AT* (Maryland Section 7), at the pilings of Sandy Hook Bridge, cross footbridge over canal. Just ahead, cross railroad tracks and reach Sandy Hook (also known, in the 19th century, as Keeptryst Post Office, after the name of a nearby mine). Turn right onto paved Sandy Hook Rd and pass under bridge. Ahead, road has almost no shoulder as it curves. *Exercise great caution.*

0.1 Bear left onto dead-end road (which formerly connected Sandy Hook Rd to US 340), cross guard rail, and ascend abandoned road. (To reach the Harpers Ferry Hostel, follow Sandy Hook Rd up hill for 0.3 mi. Hostel (with "AYH" sign) occupies house on right, at curve near top of hill.

0.2 Take pedestrian walk on downstream side of Sandy Hook Bridge (built in 1948) over Potomac River.

0.7 Maryland-Virginia state line, at south end of Sandy Hook Bridge. Follow US 340 ahead.

0.8 Va 671 intersects on left. Continue on US 340.

1.1 Trail ascends very steeply on old road into woods on left, just beyond end of guard rail.

1.3 Turn right off road and onto path just before reaching house. Ascend very steeply by switchbacks, passing several beeches.

1.6 Path on right leads a short distance to Split Rock, which offers a superb view of Harpers Ferry, Elk Ridge and the Potomac River gorge. The trail entered Harpers Ferry National Historical Park just before this point. *Camping and fires are prohibited.* Ahead, steep ascents alternate with level sections as the trail passes through hemlocks to the southeastern side of the ridge.

2.1 Path on right leads a short distance to good view under high-tension powerline.

2.3 Path on right leads a short distance to another good view from powerline. (Harpers Ferry, Bolivar, Jefferson

Rock, and the rivers are all visible; and the Alleghenies can be seen on a clear day.) Ascend gradually ahead past *profuse poison ivy* in some places. Ahead, side trail shown on map is no longer open.

2.7 Pass rock redoubts dating from the Civil War. (When Lee invaded Maryland in 1862, he detailed Jackson to capture Harpers Ferry, which fell after a short siege, Sept 13-15. Brigadier General John G. Walker's division bombarded the town from these heights. The redoubts were infantry defenses built and abandoned by the Federals.)

3.2 Junction with *AT*, in Virginia Section 1.

Detailed Trail Data—South to North

0.0 From the *AT*, in Virginia Section 1, follow ridge north. This is in Harpers Ferry National Historical Park. *Camping and fires are prohibited.*

0.1 Pass rock redoubts dating from the Civil War. (When Lee invaded Maryland in 1862, he detailed Jackson to capture Harpers Ferry, which fell after a short siege, Sept. 13-15. Brigadier General John G. Walker's division bombarded the town from these heights. The redoubts were infantry defenses built and abandoned by the Federals. Descend gradually ahead past *profuse poison ivy* in some places. Ahead, side trail shown on map is no longer open.

0.9 Path on left leads a short distance to good view from high-tension powerline clearing. (Harpers Ferry, Bolivar, Jefferson Rock, and the rivers are all visible; and the Alleghenies can be seen on a clear day.)

1.1 Path on left leads a short distance to another good view under powerline. Ahead, trail descends steeply at times, through hemlocks, to southeastern side to ridge.

1.6 Path on left leads a short distance to Split Rock, which offers a superb view of Elk Ridge, Harpers Ferry, and the Potomac River gorge. Just ahead, the trail leaves Harpers

Ferry National Historical Park and descends very steeply by switchbacks, passing several beeches.

1.9 Turn left onto old road.

2.0 Turn right off road and onto path. Ahead, turn right onto US 340.

2.4 Va 671 intersects on right. Continue on US 340.

2.5 Maryland-Virginia state line. Cross Potomac River by pedestrian walk, on right side of Sandy Hook Bridge (built in 1948).

3.0 At north end of bridge, proceed parallel to US 340 and descend on abandoned road, which formerly connected US 340 to Sandy Hook Rd.

3.1 Bear right onto paved Sandy Hook Rd. (To reach the Harpers Ferry Hostel, turn left and follow road for 0.3 mi. Hostel (with "AYH" sign) occupies house on right, at curve near top of hill. Ahead, road has almost no shoulder as it curves. *Exercise great caution.*

3.2 Sandy Hook (also known, in the 19th century, as Keeptryst Post Office, after the name of a nearby mine). Turn left off road. Ahead, cross railroad tracks and footbridge over canal to reach junction with the *AT* (Maryland Section 7), at pilings of Sandy Hook Bridge.

SKY MEADOWS STATE PARK TRAILS
Distance: 6.0 Miles

The 1,132-acre Sky Meadows State Park offers a convenient access to the *AT*, a campground, and some short circuit hikes with extraordinary views from the Park's high meadows. The trails have excellent footing and are also notable for an abundance of dogwood. The Park is open from 8 a.m. to dusk daily and has a small entrance fee per car. Beside the parking lot, the Visitor Center occupies Mt. Bleak Mansion, built about 1820 and once owned by one of Col. Mosby's rangers. In the yard stands the largest Kentucky coffee-tree in the state: 83 feet high, 7.5 feet wide, and more than 150 years old.

The campground has tent pads, a shelter, fire pits, pit toilets, and a hand-pump well (water *must* be boiled or disinfected, however). The Visitor Center (closed from Nov.-Mar.) has rest rooms available year round. The camping fee is $8.00 per site (place in fee box at campground), with a limit of six persons per site. There are no reservations; camping is on a first-come, first-served basis. Camping and fires are prohibited elsewhere in the Park.

Cross-reference: Virginia Section 4

Access: From I-66, take US 17 north; or from US 50, take US 17 south. Turn west onto Va 710, the Park entrance road.

North Ridge Trail

From Visitor Center (blue-blazed)

0.0 From road at west end of parking lot, take graveled path to left of private driveway.

0.1 Turn left onto gravel road. Ahead, turn right off road and cross stile. (Gap Run Trail goes straight from here.) Then go straight on gravel path, where Piedmont Overlook Trail intersects on right. Ascend steeply on hillside meadow with outstanding eastward view.

0.3 Bench under hickory tree.

0.5 Cross old stone wall and turn left. Level.

0.6 Ascend into open woods on dirt path. Ahead, Piedmont Overlook Trail intersects on right. Go straight and cross stile. Trail undulates ahead through red oak, hickory, and American basswood.

0.8 Descend steeply.

0.9 Bench. Gap Run Trail intersects on left. Go straight, cross creek just ahead on rock causeway, and ascend, very steeply at times.

1.0 Bear left at fork with old road.

1.4 South Ridge Trail intersects on left. Go straight.

1.7 Junction with *AT*, in Virginia Section 4.

From AT (blue-blazed)

0.0 Junction with *AT*, in Virginia Section 4. Descend, very steeply at times.

0.3 South Ridge Trail intersects on right. Go straight.

0.7 Bear right onto old road.

0.9 Cross creek on rock causeway and pass Gap Run Trail, which intersects on right. (*AT* hikers should turn right here to reach campground.) Bench. Ascend steeply ahead.

1.0 Trail undulates ahead. Pass some American basswood.

1.1 Piedmont Overlook Trail intersects on left, just past stile. Go straight. Ahead, the trail becomes graveled.

1.3 Turn right and cross old stone wall. Descend steeply on hillside meadow with outstanding eastward view.

1.4 Bench under hickory tree.

1.6 Piedmont Overlook Trail intersects on left. Go straight and turn left onto gravel road ahead.

1.7 Turn right off road and onto gravel walkway and shortly reach parking lot by Visitor Center.

Gap Run Trail

From Lower End (orange-blazed)

0.0 Lower junction with North Ridge Trail, 0.1 mi from Visitor Center. Continue straight on gravel road, where North Ridge Trail turns off road to right. Road follows an undulating lane between cow pastures.

0.3 Turn right and cross stile. (Snowden Interpretive Trail begins straight ahead.) Ahead, South Ridge Trail intersects on left. Go straight and ascend through meadow.

0.5 Cross stile and enter woods ahead.

0.6 Cross stream. Shelter and picnic tables on right. Privies on left just ahead. Well with *non-potable* water, which *must* be boiled or disinfected. Road becomes grassy ahead. Pass tent sites designated by numbered posts.

0.8 Cross creek on rock causeway and ascend steeply.

1.0 Upper junction with North Ridge Trail, at 0.9 mi from *AT*.

From Upper End (orange-blazed)

0.0 Upper junction with North Ridge Trail, at 0.9 mi from *AT*. Descend steeply.

0.3 Cross creek on rock causeway.

0.4 Pass tent sites designated by numbered posts, and pass well with *non-potable* water, which *must* be boiled or disinfected. Just ahead, privies on right and shelter and picnic tables on left.

0.5 Cross stream. Ahead, cross stile and descend through meadow.

0.7 South Ridge Trail intersects on right. Go straight.

0.8 Cross stile and turn left. Road forms an undulating lane between cow pastures. (Snowden Interpretive Trail begins to right.)

1.0 Lower junction with North Ridge Trail, 0.1 mi from Visitor Center.

Snowden Interpretive Trail

Counterclockwise Loop (silver-blazed)

0.0 Junction with Gap Run Trail. Twelve markers on this trail explain the ecology of these woods. Ascend old road originally constructed in the 1820s. Go right at fork ahead.

0.1 Descend, then level.

0.2 Ascend, then level. Undulates ahead.

0.3 Cross two bridges ahead and ascend.

0.4 Field on right.

0.5 Descend.

0.8 Cross bridge over intermittent stream. Ascend ahead.

0.9 Descend.

1.0 Turn left onto old road (Edmounds Lane). Field parallels road on right. Ascend generally.

1.1 End of loop.

South Ridge Trail

From Lower End (yellow-blazed)

0.0 Junction with Gap Run Trail.

0.1 Enter woods. Ahead, pass intersecting path and immense hickory. Ascend very steeply.

0.2 Hillside meadow with outstanding view. There is a bench a short distance up hill straight ahead. Turn left and descend. Ahead, pass path that intersects on left.

0.3 Pass ruins on left and bear right onto old road. Then pass Snowden Manor ruins on left. Stone chimney, house foundation, and well are visible. Next, turn right and skirt foot of meadow.

0.4 Turn left and ascend very steeply along edge of meadow with outstanding view.

0.5 Bench on left. Bear right around trees ahead.

0.6 Cross stile and enter woods on old road. Generally young forest ahead, with lots of grass and low weeds on each side. Ascend gradually.

1.3 Pass old road that intersects on right. Ahead, cross stream.

1.6 Junction with North Ridge Trail.

From Upper End (yellow-blazed)

0.0 Junction with North Ridge Trail. Descend gradually ahead on old road that is rapidly greening over.

0.2 Cross stream.

0.3 Bear right at fork with old road. Generally young forest ahead with lots of grass and low weeds on each side.

1.0 Cross stile and enter hillside meadow with outstanding view. Bear left around trees and skirt left edge of meadow.

1.1 Bench on right. Continue along edge of meadow and descend very steeply.

1.2 Turn right at foot of meadow and skirt edge.

1.3 Turn left into woods and descend on old road. Pass Snowden Manor ruins on right. Stone chimney, house foundation, and well are visible. Ahead, go left at fork off road and onto path. Pass more ruins on right and ascend past intersecting path on right.

1.4 Hillside meadow with outstanding view. Bench is a short distance up hill to left. Turn right and descend very steeply into woods along creek.

1.5 Pass immense hickory. Bear right at fork. Ahead, leave woods on gravel path at foot of meadow.

1.6 Junction with Gap Run Trail.

Piedmont Overlook Trail

From Lower End (red-blazed)

0.0 Lower junction with North Ridge Trail, at 0.1 mi from Visitor Center. Parallel fence. In 30 yd, turn left onto road, which curves up to open ridge and disappears. Follow cut path and posts up ridge-meadow.

0.4 Two benches at top of meadow, which has broadest view in Park. Turn left.

0.5 Bear left along fence.

0.6 Upper junction with North Ridge Trail, at 1.1 mi from *AT*.

From Upper End (red-blazed)

0.0 Junction with North Ridge Trail, at 1.1 mi from *AT*. Ascend along fence.

0.1 Bear right away from fence and come to two benches on hillside meadow, which has broadest view in Park. Descend steeply through center of meadow, following cut path and posts. Near bottom, path bears right and turns into a road, which curves back to left.

0.5 Turn right off road and follow fence.

0.6 Lower junction with North Ridge Trail, at 0.1 mi from Visitor Center.

Virginia Blue Ridge

Jim and Molly Denton Shelter

CHAPTER 9
SHELTERS

Hikers of this section of the *AT* are fortunate in having well-built and attractively located shelters that are an easy-to-moderate day's walk apart. Hikers will find that they often have the opportunity to choose their shelters according to the distance they prefer to hike.

These shelters are generally three-sided structures with raised wooden floors. Most have fireplaces and pit toilets. (Exceptions are noted in the Trail sections.) The spring at Rocky Run is seasonal.

Shelters are open to hikers for free on a first-come, first-served basis, *but early arrivals should admit latecomers up to the capacity of the shelter.* Users are expected not to deface the shelters, tables, fireplaces, etc., and they should carry out all of their trash.

Some animals in Maryland and northern Virginia, particularly raccoons, may carry rabies. Leaving behind garbage or unused food, which attracts animals, is therefore especially hazardous to the welfare of other hikers. For more information on rabies, see Chapter 1.

Caution should be used at all times with fires, which should be confined to the fireplaces and never left untended. Fires should be out to the last spark before hikers leave the shelter.

Firewood is a problem near most of the shelters, but a little scouting through the woods generally will turn up enough dry wood. In no event are standing trees (live or dead) to be cut or defaced. Hikers also are asked to leave a small supply of dry wood inside for others, who may arrive late at night or in a storm. The courtesy will be returned.

On the following list, the distances shown are from the preceding shelter, north to south. Distances do not include the length of the shelter-access trails.

State/Section	Shelter	Distance
Maryland		
1	Devils Racecourse (from Deer Lick Shelter in Penna.)	9.7
3	Hemlock Hill	4.5
3	Pine Knob	7.7
5	Rocky Run	7.4
5	Crampton Gap	4.9
Virginia		
2	David Lesser	19.7
2	Hodgson House (Blackburn Trail Center)	3.3
3	Sam Moore	10.8
3	Rod Hollow	6.9
4	Dick's Dome	9.0
4	Manassas Gap	4.4
5	Jim and Molly Denton	5.5
6	Tom Floyd Wayside	8.1

185

INDEX

This index covers only place names and road crossings that pertain to the Trail and side trails. Appalachian Mountains, Blue Ridge, South Mountain, states, and counties are omitted.